D0481486

Asian American Literature

PRENTICE HALL
Upper Saddle River, New Jersey
Needham, Massachusetts

ISBN 0-13-435467-2

5 6 7 8 9 10   02 01 00

PRENTICE HALL

Acknowledgments

Grateful acknowledgment is made to the following for copyrighted material:

The Bancroft Library
"The Piece of Straw" from *The Dancing Kettle and Other Japanese Folk Tales*, retold by Yoshiko Uchida. Copyright 1949. Courtesy of the Bancroft Library, University of California, Berkeley.

Boa Editions
"Eating Together" and "I Ask My Mother to Sing" copyright © 1986 by Li-Young Lee. Reprinted from *Rose* with the permission of BOA Editions, Ltd., 260 East Avenue, Rochester, NY 14604.

The Caxton Printers, Ltd.
"Slant-Eyed Americans" from *Yokohama, California* by Toshio Mori. Copyright 1949. Published by The Caxton Printers, Ltd., Caldwell, ID 83605. Reprinted by permission of the publisher.

Sucheng Chan
"You're Short, Besides" by Sucheng Chan. Copyright © 1989 by Sucheng Chan. Originally published in *Making Waves: An Anthology of Writings By and About Asian American Women*, edited by Asian Women United of California (Boston: Beacon Press, 1989). Reprinted by permission of the author.

Diana Chang
"Foreign Ways" and "Saying Yes" by Diana Chang. Copyrighted by Diana Chang. Reprinted by permission of the author.

Isabelle C. Chang
"The Artist" from *Tales of Old China* by Isabelle C. Chang. Copyright © 1969 by Isabelle C. Chang.

Darhansoff & Verrill Literary Agency
"Kubota" by Garrett Hongo. First published in *Ploughshares*, Copyright © 1990 by Garrett Hongo. Reprinted by permission.

Sandra Dijkstra Literary Agency
"Fish Cheeks" by Amy Tan. Copyright © 1987 by Amy Tan. First appeared in *Seventeen Magazine*. Reprinted by permission of Amy Tan and the Sandra Dijkstra Literary Agency.

(Acknowledgments continue on p. 159.)

Contents

Introduction

You may have a romantic image of explorers who risk their lives to discover new and unknown lands. Writers, too, are explorers. They may not take physical risks, but they take emotional ones as they explore their cultural backgrounds and their own hearts.

Recently, many American writers with diverse backgrounds have been opening up new heart-territory for readers. In stories, essays, and poems, writers have discovered and described what it means to be a Native American, a Mexican American, an African American, or an Asian American. Their imaginative journeys have enriched our literature.

This anthology contains the writing of Asian Americans. Much of this work appeared in the last fifteen or twenty years, and almost all of it shows Asian Americans discovering who they are and how they fit in to American society. Even a story like Lensey Namioka's "LAFFF," an entertaining science-fiction piece, touches on ways in which Chinese American students are stereotyped.

The term *Asian American* can be misleading, however, if it suggests a single group of people with the same heritage and the same reactions to American life. As you read this anthology, you'll find that there is diversity within diversity. An Asian American is someone who comes (or whose parents or forebears have come) from any number of different Asian countries. If America is a rainbow of cultures, then Asian Americans compose a mini-rainbow all their own.

In reading this volume, you'll encounter Chinese Americans like Jade Snow Wong, Japanese Americans like Lawson Fusao Inada, Vietnamese Americans like Le Ly Hayslip, and Indian Americans like Ved Mehta. You'll also encounter writers who come from a multi-ethnic background. The poet Cathy Song, for example, was born of a Chinese American mother and a Korean American father.

This diversity of backgrounds can prompt writers to focus on different historical events. For Vietnamese Americans like Le Ly Hayslip and Tran Thi Nga, the Vietnam War (which ended in 1975) is the key to their identity. Each of them grew up in Vietnam, suffered physical and emotional pain in the war, and eventually put down new roots in America. In their writing, however, they naturally return to their haunting wartime experiences to understand who they are.

Many of the Japanese American writers in this anthology discover meaning in events that occurred during World War II. December 7, 1941, the day that Japanese planes bombed Pearl Harbor, marked the beginning of an especially difficult period for Japanese Americans. Suspected of being traitors merely because of their heritage, they were taken from their schools, their jobs, and their homes and forced to live in special relocation centers. This deeply humiliating experience is reflected in the story "Slant-Eyed Americans" by Toshio Mori; essays by Monica Sone, Jeanne Wakatsuki Houston, and Garrett Hongo; and the poem "Concentration Constellation" by Lawson Fusao Inada.

Some of the Chinese American writers in this volume refer to experiences that occurred before the United States entered World War II. During the period 1910 to 1940, Chinese immigrants coming to America were detained on Angel Island in San Francisco Bay. There they met with a cold welcome. As Marlon K. Hom describes, the immigrants "had to submit to a battery of physical examinations and harsh interrogations." Hom has translated the graffiti-poems that ordinary Chinese scribbled on the walls of their detention barracks as they waited to be admitted to this country or returned to China. Many contemporary Chinese poets are too young to have experienced Angel Island for themselves. Like Alan Chong Lau, however, they can imagine what it was like for their grandparents.

Although Asian American writers are divided by different historical concerns, they are united in their treatment of universal themes. Chief among these themes is the joy of discovering one's heritage and of paying tribute to one's parents or grandparents. In his essay "Kubota," Garrett Hongo restores the good name of his Japanese grandfather, once suspected of being a spy. In his poem "I Ask My Mother to Sing," Li-Young Lee honors his mother and grandmother as they re-create for him a China he has never seen. You'll find this same theme reflected in many of the stories, essays, and poems in this book.

If you take a risk and journey with these writer-explorers, you many discover scents, tastes, sounds, and sights of cultures that are new to you. You may also discover new thoughts and feelings in your own heart.

The Explosion in the Parlor

Bai Xiao-Yi

THE host poured tea into the cup and placed it on the small table in front of his guests, who were a father and daughter, and put the lid on the cup with a clink. Apparently thinking of something, he hurried into the inner room, leaving the Thermos on the table. His two guests heard a chest of drawers opening and a rustling.

They remained sitting in the parlor, the ten-year-old daughter looking at the flowers outside the window, the father just about to take his cup, when the crash came, right there in the parlor. Something was hopelessly broken.

It was the Thermos, which had fallen to the floor. The girl looked over her shoulder abruptly, startled, staring. It was mysterious. Neither of them had touched it, not even a little bit. True, it hadn't stood steadily when their host placed it on the table, but it hadn't fallen then.

The crash of the Thermos caused the host, with a box of sugar cubes in his hand, to rush back from the inner room. He gawked at the steaming floor and blurted out, "It doesn't matter! It doesn't matter!"

The father started to say something. Then he muttered, "Sorry, I touched it and it fell."

"It doesn't matter," the host said.

Later, when they left the house, the daughter said, "Daddy, *did* you touch it?"

"No. But it stood so close to me."

"But you *didn't* touch it. I saw your reflection in the windowpane. You were sitting perfectly still."

The father laughed. "What then would you give as the cause of its fall?"

"The Thermos fell by itself. The floor is uneven. It wasn't steady when Mr. Li put it there. Daddy, *why* did you say that you . . ."

"That won't do, girl. It sounds more acceptable when I say I knocked it down. There are things which people accept less the more you defend them. The truer the story you tell, the less true it sounds."

The daughter was lost in silence for a while. Then she said, "Can you explain it only this way?"

"Only this way," her father said.

The Artist: A Chinese Fable

Isabelle C. Chang

THERE was once a king who loved the graceful curves of the rooster. He asked the court artist to paint a picture of a rooster for him. For one year he waited, and still this order was not fulfilled. In a rage, he stomped into the artist's studio and demanded to see the artist.

Quickly the artist brought out paper, paint, and brush. In five minutes a perfect picture of a rooster emerged from his skillful brush. The king turned purple with anger, saying, "If you can paint a perfect picture of a rooster in five minutes, why did you keep me waiting for over a year?"

"Come with me," begged the artist. He led the king to his storage room. Paper was piled from the floor to the ceiling. On every sheet was a painting of a rooster.

"Your Majesty," explained the artist, "it took me more than a year to learn how to paint a perfect rooster in five minutes."

Life is short, art is long.

Housepainting

Lan Samantha Chang

THE day before my sister brought her boyfriend home, we had a family conference over fried rice and Campbell's chicken noodle.

"This is the problem," my mother said. "The thistles are overpowering our mailbox." She looked at my father. "Could you do something about them before Frances and Wei get here?"

My father grunted from behind his soup. He drank his Campbell's Chinese-style, with the bowl raised to his mouth. "Frances won't care about the thistles," he said. "She thinks only about coming home."

"But what about Wei?" my mother said. "This isn't his home. To him it's just a house that hasn't been painted in ten years. With weeds." She scowled. To her the weeds were a matter of honor. Although Wei had been dating my sister for four years and had visited us three times, he was technically a stranger and subject to the rules of "saving face."

My father slurped. "Frances is a *xiaoxun* daughter," he said. "She wants to see family, not our lawn. Wei is a good *xiaoxun* boy. He wants Frances to see her family; he doesn't care about the lawn."

Xiaoxun means "filial," or "dutiful to one's parents."

I was almost to the bottom of my bowl of rice when I noticed my parents were looking at me. "Oh," I said. "Okay, I'll do it."

"Thank you, Annie," said my mother.

The next afternoon I went to work on the weeds. My father loved Wei and Frances, but he hated yard work. Whenever I read about Asian gardeners, I thought my father must have come over on a different boat.

It was a beautiful midwestern afternoon, sunny and dry, with small white clouds high up against a bright blue sky. I wore a pair of my father's old gloves to pull the thistles but kicked off my sandals, curled my toes around the hot reassuring dirt. Inside the house, my mother napped with the air conditioner humming in the window. My father sat in front of the television, rereading the Chinese newspaper from New York that my parents always snatched out of the mail as if they were receiving news of the emperor from a faraway province. I felt an invisible

4

hand hovering over our shabby blue house, making sure everything stayed the same.

I was hacking at a milky dandelion root when I heard an en-
gine idling. A small brown car, loaded down with boxes and luggage, turned laboriously into the driveway. Through the open
window I heard a scrape as my father pushed aside his footrest.
My mother's window shade snapped up and she peered outside,
one hand on her tousled hair. I rose to meet the car, conscious
of my dirt-stained feet, sweaty glasses, and muddy gardening
gloves.

"Annie!" Frances shouted from the rolled-down window. She
half-emerged from the car and shouted my name again.

"Wow," I said. "You guys are early. I thought you wouldn't get
here until five o'clock."

"That was the plan," said Wei, "but your sister here was so excited about getting home that I begged off from call a few hours
early." He grinned. He was always showing off about how well he
knew my sister. But other than that he had very few defects,
even to my critical thirteen-year-old mind. He was medium-sized
and steady, with a broad, cheerful dark face and one gold-
rimmed tooth.

My mother and father rushed out the front door and let it slam.
"Hi, Frances!" they said. "Hi, Wei!" I could tell my mother had
stopped to comb her hair and put on lipstick.

We stood blinking foolishly in the sunlight as Wei and
Frances got out of the car. My family does not hug. It is one of
the few traditions that both my parents have preserved from
China's pre-Revolutionary times.

Frances came and stood in front of my mother. "Let me look
at you," my mother said. Her gaze ran over my sister in a way
that made me feel knobby and extraneous.

Frances was as beautiful as ever. She did not look like she
had been sitting in a car all day. Her white shorts and her flowered shirt were fresh, and her long black hair rippled gently
when she moved her head. People were always watching
Frances, and Wei was no exception. Now he stared transfixed,
waiting for her to turn to talk to him, but she did not.

Still facing my mother, Frances said, "Wei, could you get the
stuff from the car?"

"I'll help you!" my father said. He walked around the back of
the car and stood awkwardly aside to let Wei open the trunk.
"So, how is medical school?" I heard him ask. They leaned into

the trunk, their conversation muffled by the hood. I looked at their matching shorts, polo shirts, brown arms and sturdy legs. When Wei came to visit, my father always acted like a caged animal that has been let outside to play with another of its kind.

Afterward, we sat in the kitchen and drank icy sweet green-bean porridge from rice bowls. Frances nudged me.

"Hey, Annie, I got you something."

She pulled a package wrapped in flowered paper from a shopping bag. She never came home without presents for everyone, and she never left without a bag full of goodies from home. It was as if she could maintain a strong enough sense of connection to us only by touching things that had actually belonged, or would soon belong, to us.

I looked at the package: a book. I stifled a groan. Frances never knew what I wanted.

"Well, open it," my mother said.

I tore off the paper. It was a thick volume about the history of medicine. This was supposed to be of great interest to me, because of a family notion that I would become a doctor, like Wei. I did not want to be a doctor.

"This is great! Thanks, Frances," I said.

"Very nice," said my mother.

"Ma, I left your present in my room," Frances said. "Let's go get it." They left the kitchen. My father and Wei began a heated discussion about Wimbledon. After a few minutes, I got bored and went to find my mother and Frances.

From the entrance to the hall I could see that the bedroom door was closed. I stopped walking and snuck up to the door on the balls of my feet. I crouched against the door to listen.

"I don't *know*, Mom," Frances was saying. She sounded close to tears.

"What is it that you don't know?" my mother asked her. When my mother got upset, her sentences became more formal and her Chinese accent more obvious. "Are you unsure that he really cares about you, or are you unsure about your feelings for him?"

"I know he cares about me," she said. She had answered my mother's question. There followed a pause in the conversation.

Then my mother said, "Well, I think he is a very nice boy. Daddy likes him very much."

"And of course that's the most important thing," said my sister, her anger startling me. I wrapped my arms around my knees.

"You know that is not true." My mother sounded exasperated. "Your father enjoys spending time with other men, that is all. There aren't very many Chinese men in this area for him to talk to. He also likes Wei because he is capable of giving you the kind of life we have always wanted you to have. Is there something . . ." She paused. "What is wrong with him?"

Frances burst into a sob.

"There's nothing *wrong* with him. There's *nothing* wrong with him. It's just—oh, I just don't know—I don't know." She was almost shouting, as if my mother didn't understand English. "You and Dad don't think about me at *all!*"

I imagined my mother's face, thin and tight, frozen in the light from the window. "Don't speak to me that way," she said stiffly. "I am only trying to help you decide. You are very young. You have never lived through a war. You don't know about the hardships of life as much as your father and I do."

"I'm *sorry*," my sister said, and sobbed even louder. I got up and snuck away down the hall.

My parents often mentioned the war, especially when I complained about doing something I didn't want to do. If I couldn't get a ride to the swimming pool, my mother told me about when *she* was in seventh grade and had to walk to school every day past a lot of dead bodies. My mother was a brave seventh grader who knew how to shoot a gun and speak four dialects. But what did I know? I'd lived in the Midwest my whole life. I ate Sugar Pops and drank milk from a cow. To me, an exciting time meant going downtown to the movies without my parents.

That night Wei and Frances and I went to a movie starring Kevin Costner and a blond woman whose name I don't remember. On the way to the theater the car was very quiet. When we arrived, I stood in line to get popcorn and then went into the dim, virtually empty theater to look for Wei and Frances. I saw them almost immediately. They were quarreling. Wei kept trying to take Frances's hand, and she kept snatching it away. As I approached, I heard him say, "Just tell me what you want from me. What do you want?"

"I don't know!" Frances said. I approached. She looked up. "Mmm—popcorn! Sit down, Annie. I have to go to the bathroom." Her look said: Don't you dare say a word.

I watched her hurry up the aisle. "What's wrong with her?"

Wei shook his head a minute, trying to dislodge an answer.

"I don't know." My first time alone with him. We sat staring awkwardly at the empty screen. Then he turned to me as if struck by an important thought.

"Annie, what would *you* think if Francie and I got married?"

Despite what I had overheard between Frances and my mother, my stomach gave a little jump. I thought about what to say.

"That would be nice," I said.

"You think so?" Wei said eagerly. "Listen, can you tell her that? I've got to convince her. It's like she can't make up her own mind. Why do you think that is?"

"I don't know," I said. "I guess she hasn't had much practice." Although I'd never thought about it before, I knew that I was right. *Xiaoxun* meant that your parents made up your mind. I pictured Wei wrapped up in flowered paper, another gift my sister brought back and forth.

Wei sat sunk in his seat, a speculative look on his face. "Hmm," he said. "Hmm."

I began to feel uncomfortable, as if I were sitting next to a mad scientist. "I can't wait to see this movie," I said quickly. "Frances and I think Kevin Costner is cute." I stuffed a handful of popcorn into my mouth. While I was chewing, Frances finally came back and sat down between us.

"How about it, Frances?" Wei said. "Do you think Kevin Costner is cute?"

I looked at Wei's face and suddenly realized that he could not look more different from Kevin Costner.

"Actually, Frances doesn't like him," I blurted out. "I just—"

At that moment the screen lit up, and despite myself, I gave an audible sigh of relief.

My father was waiting for us when we got home, under the lamp with the Chinese newspaper, in his sagging easy chair. This habit of waiting had always infuriated Frances, who felt compelled by guilt to return at a reasonable hour.

Wei greeted my father cheerfully. "Hi, Mr. Wang. Waiting up for us?"

"Oh no," my father said, regarding Wei with pleasure.

"I'm glad you're still up," Wei said, with a look of heavy male significance. "I wanted to talk to you about something."

This time I had no desire to listen in on the conversation. I headed for the bathroom as fast as I could. Frances hurried behind me.

"Aren't you going to talk with them?" I said.

Frances grabbed the doorknob. "Just shut up," she said. She closed the door behind us, and we stood for a minute in the pink-tiled room under the glow of the ceiling light. Frances leaned against the counter and sighed. I sat down on the toilet seat.

"You know," she muttered, "I really do think Kevin Costner is cute."

"Me too," I said. I stared at the tiny speckle pattern on the floor tiles.

From the kitchen we heard a burble of laughter.

"Dad really likes Wei," I said.

Frances sighed. "It's not just Dad. Mom likes him too. She's just too diplomatic to show it. Dad is more obvious." She raised her eyebrows. "At least I know exactly where I stand with Dad."

Her words frightened me.

"I don't get it," I burst out in spite of myself. "Why did you go out with him for four years if you don't really like him?"

Frances ran her hand around a water faucet. "He reminded me of home," she said. "Why did you sign up for biology instead of art class?" She slid quickly off the counter. "Come on, kiddo, time to hit the sack."

The next morning I slept late. Around eleven I was awakened by a muffled bang near my bedroom window. My mind whirled like a pinwheel: What on earth—? I jumped out of bed and pushed up the bottom of the shade.

Two male legs, clad in shorts, stood on a ladder to the right of my window. Then Wei bent down, his smile startling me.

He was holding a paintbrush.

"What are you doing?" I almost shrieked.

"Just giving your father a little help with the house," he said.

I pulled the shade down, grabbed some clothes, and hurried out of my room to find my mother. As I passed Frances's room, I saw her sitting on her bed, fully dressed, with a completely blank expression on her face.

My mother was in the kitchen, cutting canned bamboo shoots into long thin strips.

"Where is Dad?"

"Don't shout, Annie," she said. "He went to the hardware store to match some more paint."

"Why is Wei painting the house?"

My mother lined up a handful of bamboo shoots and began cutting them into cubes. "He's just being helpful."

"Why is Dad letting him be so helpful?" I couldn't find the right question. Wei must have asked my father if he needed help with the house. Why had my father consented? Why was he accepting help from an outsider?

My mother turned and looked at me. "Because Wei wanted to help, that's all. Why don't you go and wash up? You're thirteen years old; I shouldn't have to remind you to wash your face."

The next few days passed in a blur, marked only by the growing patch of fresh pale-yellow paint that grew to cover one side of our blue house and then the back. Wei worked steadily and cheerfully, with minimal help from my father. My mother went outside now and then to give him cold drinks and to comment on the evenness of his job, or something like that. Frances stayed in her room reading. I reported to her.

"Wei's finished with the back side and now he's starting on the garage," I said.

"Leave me alone," Frances said.

I went further into the room and stood in front of her until she looked up. "I said leave me *alone*, Annie! I'm warning you—"

"Well, why don't *you* say something about it?" I demanded. "Why didn't you tell him you didn't want him to do it?"

Her face contorted in something between anger and tears. "I can't tell him! He won't listen to me! He says he's just doing them a favor!" She bent over her book and flipped her hair angrily in front of her, shielding her face. "Go away!"

I left the room.

With things at home going so well, my parents left the next morning on a day trip to Chicago. Every now and then they made the four-hour drive to buy supplies—dried mushrooms, canned vegetables—from a Chinese grocery there. After they left, we ate breakfast, with Wei and I making awkward conversation because Frances wouldn't talk to us. Then Wei got up and went out to the front yard. From an open window I watched him pry the lid off a can of paint and stir with a wooden stick from the hardware store. Frances went out on the front porch and stood at the top of the steps looking down at him.

"You can stop now, Wei," I heard her say.

He glanced up, puzzled.

"You don't have to paint today. Mom and Dad aren't around

to see what a dutiful boy you are."

Wei didn't have a short fuse. He shook his head slowly and looked back down at what he was doing.

Frances tried again. "It makes me sick," she said, "to see you groveling like this around my parents."

Wei didn't answer.

"What is it with you?" she sneered.

Finally his eyes flickered. "My painting the house," he said, "is something between me and your parents. If you don't like it, why don't you go pick a fight with them? And why did you wait until they left to pick a fight with me?"

Frances's upper lip pulled back toward her nose. I thought she was sneering at him again, but when she turned back to the house, I realized she was crying. She looked horrible. She slammed the door, rushed past me, and ran into the garage, where she and Wei had parked the brown car. Then before Wei and I could stop her, she drove away down the street.

She came back in about an hour. I sat inside pretending to read a book, but Frances didn't reenter the house, so I figured she and Wei were talking out there. I was surprised when he came inside. "Where's Frances?" he said.

"I thought she was with you."

"Nope. Just finished the front. I'm about to put a second coat on the south side. Want to take a look?"

"Okay." I put down my book. We walked outside and around the house.

There stood Frances with her hair up in a painter's cap, busily putting blue back over Wei's work, painting fast, as high as she could reach. Two new cans stood in the grass. She had finished most of the side and had worked almost up to the corner.

Frances turned to look at us. There were splotches of blue paint on her hands and clothes.

"I liked it better the old way," she said. She glared at Wei, waiting for him to get angry, but he stood perfectly still. I felt cool sweat break out on my neck and forehead.

Finally Wei said, "If you wanted it blue again, you just had to tell me."

Frances threw her brush on the ground and burst into tears. "Damn you!" she shouted at Wei. "I hate you! You too, Annie! I hate both of you! I hate everything!" She looked at the house. "I don't care what color it is, I just hate everything!"

I took a step backward, but Wei walked right up to her and

put his hand on her shoulder. Frances hid her face in her hands and sobbed. They stood like that for a long time, Frances crying and mumbling under her breath, and then she began to repeat one sentence over and over. I leaned forward, straining to make it out.

"Mom and Dad are going to *kill* me."

Wei looked relieved. "If we all start now, we can probably paint yellow over it before they get home," he said.

Two days later Wei finished the house. He and my father drove to the hardware store to buy white paint for the trim. I was sitting in the family room, listlessly leafing through a *Time* magazine, when Frances stopped in the door.

"Hey, Annie. Wanna go out and take a look?"

"Okay," I said, surprised by her sudden friendliness.

We walked out the front door, crossed the street, and stood facing the house. The street lamps had just turned on, and the house glowed gently in the twilight. Our raggedy lawn and messy garden were hidden in the shadows.

We stood for some time, and then Frances said, "I told Wei that I would marry him."

I looked at her. Her face was expressionless in the glow from the street lamp. Finally she turned and briefly met my eyes.

"It's not worth the trouble," she said. "Let's not talk about it anymore, okay?"

"Okay," I said. Without talking, we crossed the street and approached the house. It was a beautiful evening. My mother stood behind the kitchen window, washing the dishes. Frances walked smoothly at my side, her long hair flowing back in the dusk. I glanced up at the roof in a hopeful way, but the imaginary hand that had hovered over our home had disappeared. I blinked my eyes a couple of times and looked again, but it was gone.

"Come on, Annie," my sister said, holding the door. "Hurry up, or the mosquitoes will get in."

I took a deep breath and went inside.

The White Umbrella

Gish Jen

WHEN I was twelve, my mother went to work without telling me or my little sister.

"Not that we need the second income." The lilt of her accent drifted from the kitchen up to the top of the stairs, where Mona and I were listening.

"No," said my father, in a barely audible voice. "Not like the Lee family."

The Lees were the only other Chinese family in town. I remembered how sorry my parents had felt for Mrs. Lee when she started waitressing downtown the year before; and so when my mother began coming home late, I didn't say anything, and tried to keep Mona from saying anything either.

"But why shouldn't I?" she argued. "Lots of people's mothers work."

"Those are American people," I said.

"So what do you think we are? I can do the pledge of allegiance with my eyes closed."

Nevertheless, she tried to be discreet; and if my mother wasn't home by 5:30, we would start cooking by ourselves, to make sure dinner would be on time. Mona would wash the vegetables and put on the rice; I would chop.

For weeks we wondered what kind of work she was doing. I imagined that she was selling perfume, testing dessert recipes for the local newspaper. Or maybe she was working for the florist. Now that she had learned to drive, she might be delivering boxes of roses to people.

"I don't think so," said Mona as we walked to our piano lesson after school. "She would've hit something by now."

A gust of wind littered the street with leaves.

"Maybe we better hurry up," she went on, looking at the sky. "It's going to pour."

"But we're too early." Her lesson didn't begin until 4:00, mine until 4:30, so we usually tried to walk as slowly as we could. "And anyway, those aren't the kind of clouds that rain. Those are cumulus clouds."

We arrived out of breath and wet.

"Oh, you poor, poor dears," said old Miss Crosman. "Why don't you call me the next time it's like this out? If your mother won't drive you, I can come pick you up."

"No, that's okay," I answered. Mona wrung her hair out on Miss Crosman's rug. "We just couldn't get the roof of our car to close, is all. We took it to the beach last summer and got sand in the mechanism." I pronounced this last word carefully, as if the credibility of my lie depended on its middle syllable. "It's never been the same." I thought for a second. "It's a convertible."

"Well then make yourselves at home." She exchanged looks with Eugenie Roberts, whose lesson we were interrupting. Eugenie smiled good-naturedly. "The towels are in the closet across from the bathroom."

Huddling at the end of Miss Crosman's nine-foot leatherette couch, Mona and I watched Eugenie play. She was a grade ahead of me and, according to school rumor, had a boyfriend in high school. I believed it. She had auburn hair, blue eyes, and, I noted with a particular pang, a pure white folding umbrella.

"I can't see," whispered Mona.

"So clean your glasses."

"My glasses *are* clean. You're in the way."

I looked at her. "They look dirty to me."

"That's because *your* glasses are dirty."

Eugenie came bouncing to the end of her piece.

"Oh! Just stupendous!" Miss Crosman hugged her, then looked up as Eugenie's mother walked in. "Stupendous!" she said again. "Oh! Mrs. Roberts! Your daughter has a gift, a real gift. It's an honor to teach her."

Mrs. Roberts, radiant with pride, swept her daughter out of the room as if she were royalty, born to the piano bench. Watching the way Eugenie carried herself, I sat up, and concentrated so hard on sucking in my stomach that I did not realize until the Robertses were gone that Eugenie had left her umbrella. As Mona began to play, I jumped up and ran to the window, meaning to call to them—only to see their brake lights flash then fade at the stop sign at the corner. As if to allow them passage, the rain had let up; a quivering sun lit their way.

The umbrella glowed like a scepter on the blue carpet while Mona, slumping over the keyboard, managed to eke out a fair rendition of a catfight. At the end of the piece, Miss Crosman asked her to stand up.

"Stay right there," she said, then came back a minute later with a towel to cover the bench. "You must be cold," she continued. "Shall I call your mother and have her bring over some dry clothes?"

"No," answered Mona. "She won't come because she . . ."

"She's too busy," I broke in from the back of the room.

"I see." Miss Crosman sighed and shook her head a little. "Your glasses are filthy, honey," she said to Mona. "Shall I clean them for you?"

Sisterly embarrassment seized me. Why hadn't Mona wiped her lenses when I told her to? As she resumed abuse of the piano, I stared at the umbrella. I wanted to open it, twirl it around by its slender silver handle; I wanted to dangle it from my wrist on the way to school the way the other girls did. I wondered what Miss Crosman would say if I offered to bring it to Eugenie at school tomorrow. She would be impressed with my consideration for others; Eugenie would be pleased to have it back; and I would have possession of the umbrella for an entire night. I looked at it again, toying with the idea of asking for one for Christmas. I knew, however, how my mother would react.

"Things," she would say. "What's the matter with a raincoat? All you want is things, just like an American."

Sitting down for my lesson, I was careful to keep the towel under me and sit up straight.

"I'll bet you can't see a thing either," said Miss Crosman, reaching for my glasses. "And you can relax, you poor dear." She touched my chest, in an area where she never would have touched Eugenie Roberts. "This isn't a boot camp."

When Miss Crosman finally allowed me to start playing I played extra well, as well as I possibly could. See, I told her with my fingers. You don't have to feel sorry for me.

"That was wonderful," said Miss Crosman. "Oh! Just wonderful."

An entire constellation rose in my heart.

"And guess what," I announced proudly. "I have a surprise for you."

Then I played a second piece for her, a much more difficult one that she had not assigned.

"Oh! That was stupendous," she said without hugging me. "Stupendous! You are a genius, young lady. If your mother had started you younger, you'd be playing like Eugenie Roberts by now!"

I looked at the keyboard, wishing that I had still a third, even more difficult piece to play for her. I wanted to tell her that I was the school spelling bee champion, that I wasn't ticklish, that I could do karate.

"My mother is a concert pianist," I said.

She looked at me for a long moment, then finally, without saying anything, hugged me. I didn't say anything about bringing the umbrella to Eugenie at school.

The steps were dry when Mona and I sat down to wait for my mother.

"Do you want to wait inside?" Miss Crosman looked anxiously at the sky.

"No," I said. "Our mother will be here any minute."

"In a while," said Mona.

"Any minute," I said again, even though my mother had been at least twenty minutes late every week since she started working.

According to the church clock across the street we had been waiting twenty-five minutes when Miss Crosman came out again.

"Shall I give you ladies a ride home?"

"No," I said. "Our mother is coming any minute."

"Shall I at least give her a call and remind her you're here? Maybe she forgot about you."

"I don't think she *forgot*," said Mona.

"Shall I give her a call anyway? Just to be safe?"

"I bet she already left," I said. "How could she forget about us?"

Miss Crosman went in to call.

"There's no answer," she said, coming back out.

"See, she's on her way," I said.

"Are you sure you wouldn't like to come in?"

"No," said Mona.

"Yes," I said. I pointed at my sister. "She meant yes too. She meant no, she wouldn't like to go in."

Miss Crosman looked at her watch. "It's 5:30 now, ladies. My pot roast will be coming out in fifteen minutes. Maybe you'd like to come in and have some then?"

"My mother's almost here," I said. "She's on her way."

We watched and watched the street. I tried to imagine what my mother was doing; I tried to imagine her writing messages in the sky, even though I knew she was afraid of planes. I watched as the branches of Miss Crosman's big willow tree started to sway; they had all been trimmed to exactly the same height off the ground, so that they looked beautiful, like hair in the wind.

It started to rain.

"Miss Crosman is coming out again," said Mona.

"Don't let her talk you into going inside," I whispered.

"Why not?"

"Because that would mean Mom isn't really coming any minute."

"But she isn't," said Mona. "She's *working*."

"Shhh! Miss Crosman is going to hear you."

"She's working! She's working! She's working!"

I put my hand over her mouth, but she licked it, and so I was wiping my hand on my wet dress when the front door opened.

"We're getting even *wetter*," said Mona right away. "Wetter and wetter."

"Shall we all go in?" Miss Crosman pulled Mona to her feet. "Before you young ladies catch pneumonia? You've been out half an hour already."

"We're *freezing*." Mona looked up at Miss Crosman. "Do you have any hot chocolate? We're going to catch *pneumonia*."

"I'm not going in," I said. "My mother's coming any minute."

"Come on," said Mona. "Use your *noggin*."

"Any minute."

"Come on, Mona," Miss Crosman opened the door. "Shall we get you inside first?"

"See you in the hospital," said Mona as she went in. "See you in the hospital with *pneumonia*."

I stared out into the empty street. The rain was pricking me all over; I was cold; I wanted to go inside. I wanted to be able to let myself go inside. If Miss Crosman came out again, I decided, I would go in.

She came out with a blanket and the white umbrella.

I could not believe that I was actually holding the umbrella, opening it. It sprang up by itself as if it were alive, as if that were what it wanted to do—as if it belonged in my hands, above my head. I stared up at the network of silver spokes, then spun the umbrella around and around and around. It was so clean and white that it seemed to glow, to illuminate everything around it.

"It's beautiful," I said.

Miss Crosman sat down next to me, on one end of the blanket. I moved the umbrella over so that it covered that too. I could feel the rain on my left shoulder and shivered. She put her arm around me.

"You poor, poor dear."

I knew that I was in store for another bolt of sympathy, and braced myself by staring up into the umbrella.

"You know, I very much wanted to have children when I was younger," she continued.

"You did?"

She stared at me a minute. Her face looked dry and crusty, like day-old frosting.

"I did. But then I never got married."

I twirled the umbrella around again.

"This is the most beautiful umbrella I have ever seen," I said. "Ever, in my whole life."

"Do you have an umbrella?"

"No. But my mother's going to get me one just like this for Christmas."

"Is she? I tell you what. You don't have to wait until Christmas. You can have this one."

"But this one belongs to Eugenie Roberts," I protested. "I have to give it back to her tomorrow in school."

"Who told you it belongs to Eugenie? It's not Eugenie's. It's mine. And now I'm giving it to you, so it's yours."

"It is?"

She hugged me tighter. "That's right. It's all yours."

"It's mine?" I didn't know what to say. "Mine?" Suddenly I was jumping up and down in the rain. "It's beautiful! Oh! It's beautiful!" I laughed.

Miss Crosman laughed too, even though she was getting all wet.

"Thank you, Miss Crosman. Thank you very much. Thanks a zillion. It's beautiful. It's *stupendous*!"

"You're quite welcome," she said.

"Thank you," I said again, but that didn't seem like enough. Suddenly I knew just what she wanted to hear. "I wish you were my mother."

Right away I felt bad.

"You shouldn't say that," she said, but her face was opening into a huge smile as the lights of my mother's car cautiously turned the corner. I quickly collapsed the umbrella and put it up my skirt, holding onto it from the outside, through the material.

"Mona!" I shouted into the house. "Mona! Hurry up! Mom's here! I told you she was coming!"

Then I ran away from Miss Crosman, down to the curb. Mona came tearing up to my side as my mother neared the house. We both backed up a few feet, so that in case she went onto the curb, she wouldn't run us over.

"But why didn't you go inside with Mona?" my mother asked on the way home. She had taken off her own coat to put over me, and had the heat on high.

"She wasn't using her noggin," said Mona, next to me in the back seat.

"I should call next time," said my mother. "I just don't like to say where I am."

That was when she finally told us that she was working as a check-out clerk in the A&P. She was supposed to be on the day shift, but the other employees were unreliable, and her boss had promised her a promotion if she would stay until the evening shift filled in.

For a moment no one said anything. Even Mona seemed to find the revelation disappointing.

"A promotion already!" she said, finally.

I listened to the windshield wipers.

"You're so quiet." My mother looked at me in the rear view mirror. "What's the matter?"

"I wish you would quit," I said after a moment.

She sighed. "The Chinese have a saying: one beam cannot hold the roof up."

"But Eugenie Roberts's father supports their family."

She sighed once more. "Eugenie Roberts's father is Eugenie Roberts's father," she said.

As we entered the downtown area, Mona started leaning hard against me every time the car turned right, trying to push me over. Remembering what I had said to Miss Crosman, I tried to maneuver the umbrella under my leg so she wouldn't feel it.

"What's under your skirt?" Mona wanted to know as we came to a traffic light. My mother, watching us in the rear view mirror again, rolled slowly to a stop.

"What's the matter?" she asked.

"There's something under her skirt!" said Mona, pulling at me.

"Under her skirt?"

Meanwhile, a man crossing the street started to yell at us. "Who do you think you are, lady?" he said. "You're blocking the whole crosswalk."

We all froze. Other people walking by stopped to watch.

"Didn't you hear me?" he went on, starting to thump on the hood with his fist. "Don't you speak English?"

My mother began to back up, but the car behind us honked. Luckily, the light turned green right after that. She sighed in relief.

"What were you saying, Mona?" she asked.

We wouldn't have hit the car behind us that hard if he hadn't been moving too, but as it was our car bucked violently, throwing us all first back and then forward.

"Uh oh," said Mona when we stopped. "*Another* accident."

I was relieved to have attention diverted from the umbrella. Then I noticed my mother's head, tilted back onto the seat. Her eyes were closed.

"Mom!" I screamed. "Mom! Wake up!"

She opened her eyes. "Please don't yell," she said. "Enough people are going to yell already."

"I thought you were dead," I said, starting to cry. "I thought you were dead."

She turned around, looked at me intently, then put her hand on my forehead.

"Sick," she confirmed. "Some kind of sick is giving you crazy ideas."

As the man from the car behind us started tapping on the window, I moved the umbrella away from my leg. Then Mona and my mother were getting out of the car. I got out after them; and while everyone else was inspecting the damage we'd done, I threw the umbrella down a sewer.

Slant-Eyed Americans

Toshio Mori

MY mother was commenting on the fine California weather. It was Sunday noon, December 7. We were having our lunch, and I had the radio going.

"Let's take the afternoon off and go to the city," I said to Mother.

"All right. We shall go," she said dreamily. "Ah, four months ago my boy left Hayward to join the army, and a fine send-off he had. Our good friends—ah, I shall never forget the day of his departure."

"We'll visit some of our friends in Oakland and then take in a movie," I said. "Care to come along, Papa?"

Father shook his head. "No, I'll stay home and take it easy."

"That's his heaven," Mother commented. "To stay home, read the papers over and over, and smoke his Bull Durham."

I laughed. Suddenly the musical program was cut off as a special announcement came over the air: At 7:25 a.m. this morning a squadron of Japanese bombing planes attacked Pearl Harbor. The battle is still in progress.

"What's this? Listen to the announcement," I cried, going to the radio.

Abruptly the announcement stopped and the musicale continued.

"What is it?" Mother asked. "What has happened?"

"The radio reports that the Japanese planes attacked Hawaii this morning," I said incredulously. "It couldn't be true."

"It must be a mistake. Couldn't it have been a part of a play?" asked Mother.

I dialed other stations. Several minutes later one of the stations confirmed the bulletin.

"It must be true," Father said quietly.

I said, "Japan has declared war on the United States and Great Britain."

The room became quiet but for the special bulletin coming in every now and then.

"It cannot be true, yet it must be so," Father said over and over.

"Can it be one of those programs scaring the people about invasion?" Mother asked me.

"No, I'm sure this is a news report," I replied.

Mother's last ray of hope paled and her eyes became dull. "Why did it have to happen? The common people in Japan don't want war, and we don't want war. Here the people are peace-loving. Why cannot the peoples of the earth live together peacefully?"

"Since Japan declared war on the United States it'll mean that you parents of American citizens have become enemy aliens," I said.

"Enemy aliens," my mother whispered.

Night came but sleep did not come. We sat up late in the night hoping against hope that some good news would come, retracting the news of vicious attack and open hostilities.

"This is very bad for the people with Japanese faces," I said.

Father slowly shook his head.

"What shall we do?" asked Mother.

"What can we do?" Father said helplessly.

At the flower market next morning the growers were present but the buyers were scarce. The place looked empty and deserted. "Our business is shot to pieces," one of the boys said.

"Who'll buy flowers now?" another called.

Don Haley, the seedsman, came over looking bewildered. "I suppose you don't need seeds now."

We shook our heads.

"It looks bad," I said. "Will it affect your business?"

"Flower seed sale will drop but the vegetable seeds will move quicker," Don said. "I think I'll have to put more time on the vegetable seeds."

Nobu Hiramatsu who had been thinking of building another greenhouse joined us. He had plans to grow more carnations and expand his business.

"What's going to happen to your plans, Nobu?" asked one of the boys.

"Nothing. I'm going to sit tight and see how the things turn out," he said.

"Flowers and war don't go together," Don said. "You cannot concentrate too much on beauty when destruction is going about you."

"Sure, pretty soon we'll raise vegetables instead of flowers," Grasselli said.

A moment later the market opened and we went back to the tables to sell our flowers. Several buyers came in and purchased a little. The flowers didn't move at all. Just as I was about to leave the place I met Tom Yamashita, the Nisei gardener with a future.

"What are you doing here, Tom? What's the matter with your work?" I asked as I noticed his pale face.

"I was too sick with yesterday's news so I didn't work," he said. "This is the end. I am done for."

"No, you're not. Buck up, Tom," I cried. "You have a good future, don't lose hope."

"Sometimes I feel all right. You are an American, I tell myself. Devote your energy and life to the American way of life. Long before this my mind was made up to become a true American. This morning my Caucasian American friends sympathized with me. I felt good and was grateful. Our opportunity has come to express ourselves and act. We are Americans in thought and action. I felt like leaping to work. Then I got sick again because I got to thinking that Japan was the country that attacked the United States. I wanted to bury myself for shame."

I put my hand on his shoulder. "We all feel the same way, Tom. We're human so we flounder around awhile when an unexpected and big problem confronts us, but now that situation has to be passed by. We can't live in the same stage long. We have to move along, face the reality no matter what's in store for us."

Tom stood silently.

"Let's go to my house and take the afternoon off," I suggested. "We'll face a new world tomorrow morning with boldness and strength. What do you say, Tom?"

"All right," Tom agreed.

At home Mother was anxiously waiting for me. When she saw Tom with me her eyes brightened. Tom Yamashita was a favorite of my mother's.

"Look, a telegram from Kazuo!" she cried to me, holding up an envelope. "Read it and tell me what he says."

I tore it open and read. "He wants us to send $45 for train fare. He has a good chance for a furlough."

Mother fairly leaped in the air with the news. She had not seen my brother for four months. "How wonderful! This can happen only in America."

Suddenly she noticed Tom looking glum, and pushed him in the house. "Cheer up, Tom. This is no time for young folks to despair. Roll up your sleeves and get to work. America needs you."

Tom smiled for the first time and looked at me.

"See, Tom?" I said. "She's quick to recover. Yesterday she was wilted, and she's seventy-three."

"Tom, did you go to your gardens today?" she asked him.

"No."

"Why not?" she asked, and then added quickly. "You young men should work hard all the more, keeping up the normal routine of life. You ought to know, Tom, that if everybody dropped their work everything would go to seed. Who's going to take care of the gardens if you won't?"

Tom kept still.

Mother poured tea and brought the cookies. "Don't worry about your old folks. We have stayed here to belong to the American way of life. Time will tell our true purpose. We remained in America for permanence—not for temporary convenience. We common people need not fear."

"I guess you are right," Tom agreed.

"And America is right. She cannot fail. Her principles will stand the test of time and tyranny. Someday aggression will be outlawed by all nations."

Mother left the room to prepare the dinner. Tom got up and began to walk up and down the room. Several times he looked out the window and watched the wind blow over the field.

"Yes, if the gardens are ruined I'll rebuild them," he said. "I'll take charge of every garden in the city. All the gardens of America for that matter. I'll rebuild them as fast as the enemies wreck them. We'll have nature on our side and you cannot crush nature."

I smiled and nodded. "Good for you! Tomorrow we'll get up early in the morning and work, sweat, and create. Let's shake on it."

We solemnly shook hands, and by the grip of his fingers I knew he was ready to lay down his life for America and for his gardens.

"No word from him yet," Mother said worriedly. "He should have arrived yesterday. What's happened to him?"

It was eight in the evening, and we had had no word from my brother for several days.

"He's not coming home tonight. It's too late now," I said. "He should have arrived in Oakland this morning at the latest."

Our work had piled up and we had to work late into the night. There were still some pompons to bunch. Faintly the phone rang in the house.

"The phone!" cried Mother excitedly. "It's Kazuo, sure enough."

In the flurry of several minutes I answered the phone, greeted my brother, and was on my way to San Leandro to drive him home. On the way I tried to think of the many things I wanted to say. From the moment I spotted him waiting on the corner I could not say the thing I wanted to. I took his bag and he got in the car, and for some time we did not say anything. Then I asked him how the weather had been in Texas and how he had been.

"We were waiting for you since yesterday," I said. "Mother is home getting the supper ready. You haven't eaten yet, have you?"

He shook his head. "The train was late getting into Los Angeles. We were eight hours behind time and I should have reached San Francisco this morning around eight."

Reaching home it was the same way. Mother could not say anything. "We have nothing special tonight, wish we had something good."

"Anything would do, Mama," my brother said.

Father sat in the room reading the papers but his eyes were over the sheet and his hands were trembling. Mother scurried about getting his supper ready. I sat across the table from my brother, and in the silence which was action I watched the wave of emotions in the room. My brother was aware of it too. He sat there without a word, but I knew he understood. Not many years ago he was the baby of the family, having never been away from home. Now he was on his own, his quiet confidence actually making him appear larger. Keep up the fire, that was his company's motto. It was evident that he was a soldier. He had gone beyond life and death matter, where the true soldiers of war or peace must travel, and had returned.

For five short days we went about our daily task, picking and bunching the flowers for Christmas, eating heavy meals, and visiting the intimates. It was as if we were waiting for the hour of his departure, the time being so short. Every minute was crowded with privacy, friends, and nursery work. Too soon the time for his train came but the family had little to talk.

"Kazuo, don't worry about home or me," Mother said as we rode into town.

"Take care of yourself," my brother told her.

At the 16th Street Station Mother's close friend was waiting for us. She came to bid my brother good-bye. We had fifteen minutes to wait. My brother bought a copy of *The Coast* to see if his cartoons were in.

"Are you in this month's issue?" I asked.

"I haven't seen it yet," he said, leafing the pages. "Yes, I'm in. Here it is."

"Good!" I said. "Keep trying hard. Someday peace will come, and when you return laughter will reign once again."

My mother showed his cartoon to her friend. The train came in and we got up. It was a long one. We rushed to the Los Angeles-bound coach.

Mother's friend shook hands with my brother. "Give your best to America. Our people's honor depend on you Nisei soldiers."

My brother nodded and then glanced at Mother. For a moment her eyes twinkled and she nodded. He waved good-bye from the platform. Once inside the train we lost him. When the train began to move my mother cried, "Why doesn't he pull up the shades and look out? Others are doing it."

We stood and watched until the last of the train was lost in the night of darkness.

LAFFF

Lensey Namioka

IN movies, geniuses have frizzy white hair, right? They wear thick glasses and have names like Dr. Zweistein.

Peter Lu didn't have frizzy white hair. He had straight hair, as black as licorice. He didn't wear thick glasses, either, since his vision was normal.

Peter's family, like ours, had immigrated from China, but they had settled here first. When we moved into a house just two doors down from the Lus, they gave us some good advice on how to get along in America.

I went to the same school as Peter, and we walked to the school bus together every morning. Like many Chinese parents, mine made sure that I worked very hard in school.

In spite of all I could do, my grades were nothing compared to Peter's. He was at the top in all his classes. We walked to the school bus without talking because I was a little scared of him. Besides, he was always deep in thought.

Peter didn't have any friends. Most of the kids thought he was a nerd because they saw his head always buried in books. I didn't think he even tried to join the rest of us or cared what the others thought of him.

Then on Halloween he surprised us all. As I went down the block trick-or-treating, dressed as a zucchini in my green sweats, I heard a strange, deep voice behind me say, "How do you do."

I yelped and turned around. Peter was wearing a long, black Chinese gown with slits in the sides. On his head he had a little round cap, and down each side of his mouth drooped a thin, long mustache.

"I am Dr. Lu Manchu, the mad scientist," he announced, putting his hands in his sleeves and bowing.

He smiled when he saw me staring at his costume. It was a scary smile, somehow.

Some of the other kids came up, and when they saw Peter, they were impressed. "Hey, neat!" said one boy.

I hadn't expected Peter to put on a costume and go trick-or-treating like a normal kid. So maybe he did want to join the others after all—at least some of the time. After that night he wasn't a nerd anymore. He was Dr. Lu Manchu. Even some of the teachers began to call him that.

When we became too old for trick-or-treating, Peter was still Dr. Lu Manchu. The rumor was that he was working on a fantastic machine in his parents' garage. But nobody had any idea what it was.

One evening, as I was coming home from a baby-sitting job, I cut across the Lus' backyard. Passing their garage, I saw through a little window that the light was on. My curiosity got the better of me, and I peeked in.

I saw a booth that looked like a shower stall. A stool stood in the middle of the stall, and hanging over the stool was something that looked like a great big shower head.

Suddenly a deep voice behind me said, "Good evening, Angela." Peter bowed and smiled his scary smile. He didn't have his costume on and he didn't have the long, droopy mustache. But he was Dr. Lu Manchu.

"What are you doing?" I squeaked.

Still in his strange, deep voice, Peter said, "What are *you* doing? After all, this is my garage."

"I was just cutting across your yard to get home. Your parents never complained before."

"I thought you were spying on me," and Peter. "I thought you wanted to know about my machine." He hissed when he said the word *machine*.

Honestly, he was beginning to frighten me. "What machine?" I demanded. "You mean this shower-stall thing?"

He drew himself up and narrowed his eyes, making them into thin slits. "This is my time machine!"

I goggled at him. "You mean . . . you mean . . . this machine can send you forward and backward in time?"

"Well, actually, I can only send things forward in time," admitted Peter, speaking in his normal voice again. "That's why I'm calling the machine LAFFF. It stands for Lu's Artifact For Fast Forward."

Of course Peter always won first prize at the annual statewide science fair. But that's a long way from making a time machine. Minus his mustache and long Chinese gown, he was just Peter Lu.

"I don't believe it!" I said. "I bet LAFFF is only good for a laugh."

"Okay, Angela. I'll show you!" hissed Peter.

He sat down on the stool and twisted a dial. I heard some *bleeps, cheeps,* and *gurgles.* Peter disappeared.

He must have done it with mirrors. I looked around the garage. I peeked under the tool bench. There was no sign of him.

"Okay, I give up," I told him. "It's a good trick, Peter. You can come out now."

Bleep, cheep, and *gurgle* went the machine, and there was Peter, sitting on the stool. He held a red rose in his hand. "What do you think of that?"

I blinked. "So you produced a flower. Maybe you had it under the stool."

"Roses bloom in June, right?" he demanded.

That was true. And this was December.

"I sent myself forward in time to June when the flowers were blooming," said Peter. "And I picked the rose from our yard. Convinced, Angela?"

It was too hard to swallow. "You said you couldn't send things back in time," I objected. "So how did you bring the rose back?"

But even as I spoke I saw that his hands were empty. The rose was gone.

"That's one of the problems with the machine," said Peter. "When I send myself forward, I can't seem to stay there for long. I snap back to my own time after only a minute. Anything I bring with me snaps back to its own time, too. So my rose has gone back to this June."

I was finally convinced, and I began to see possibilities. "Wow, just think: If I don't want to do the dishes, I can send myself forward to the time when the dishes are already done."

"That won't do you much good," said Peter. "You'd soon pop back to the time when the dishes were still dirty."

Too bad. "There must be something your machine is good for," I said. Then I had another idea. "Hey, you can bring me back a piece of fudge from the future, and I can eat it twice: once now, and again in the future."

"Yes, but the fudge wouldn't stay in your stomach," said Peter. "It would go back to the future."

"That's even better!" I said. "I can enjoy eating the fudge over and over again without getting fat!"

It was late, and I had to go home before my parents started to worry. Before I left, Peter said, "Look, Angela, there's still a lot of work to do on LAFFF. Please don't tell anybody about the machine until I've got it right."

A few days later I asked him how he was doing.

"I can stay in the future time a bit longer now," he said. "Once I got it up to four minutes."

"Is that enough time to bring me back some fudge from the future?" I asked.

"We don't keep many sweets around the house," he said. "But I'll see what I can do."

A few minutes later, he came back with a spring roll for me. "My mother was frying these in the kitchen, and I snatched one while she wasn't looking."

I bit into the hot, crunchy spring roll, but before I finished chewing, it disappeared. The taste of soy sauce, green onions, and bean sprouts stayed a little longer in my mouth, though.

It was fun to play around with LAFFF, but it wasn't really useful. I didn't know what a great help it would turn out to be.

Every year our school held a writing contest, and the winning story for each grade got printed in our school magazine. I wanted desperately to win. I worked awfully hard in school, but my parents still thought I could do better.

Winning the writing contest would show my parents that I was really good in something. I love writing stories, and I have lots of ideas. But when I actually write them down, my stories never turn out as good as I thought. I just can't seem to find the right words, because English isn't my first language.

I got an honorable mention last year, but it wasn't the same as winning and showing my parents my name, Angela Tang, printed in the school magazine.

The deadline for the contest was getting close, and I had a pile of stories written, but none of them looked like a winner.

Then, the day before the deadline, *boing*, a brilliant idea hit me.

I thought of Peter and his LAFFF machine.

I rushed over to the Lus' garage and, just as I had hoped, Peter was there, tinkering with his machine.

"I've got this great idea for winning the story contest," I told him breathlessly. "You see, to be certain of winning, I have to write the story that would be the winner."

"That's obvious," Peter said dryly. "In fact, you're going around in a circle."

"Wait, listen!" I said. "I want to use LAFFF and go forward to the time when the next issue of the school magazine is out.

Then I can read the winning story."

After a moment Peter nodded. "I see. You plan to write down the winning story after you've read it and then send it in to the contest."

I nodded eagerly. "The story would *have* to win, because it's the winner!"

Peter began to look interested. "I've got LAFFF to the point where I can stay in the future for seven minutes now. Will that be long enough for you?"

"I'll just have to work quickly," I said.

Peter smiled. It wasn't his scary Lu Manchu smile, but a nice smile. He was getting as excited as I was. "Okay, Angela. Let's go for it."

He led me to the stool. "What's your destination?" he asked. "I mean, *when's* your destination?"

Suddenly I was nervous. I told myself that Peter had made many time trips, and he looked perfectly healthy.

Why not? What have I got to lose—except time?

I took a deep breath. "I want to go forward three weeks in time." By then I'd have a copy of the new school magazine in my room.

"Ready, Angela?" asked Peter.

"As ready as I'll ever be," I whispered.

Beep, cheep, and *gurgle.* Suddenly Peter disappeared.

What went wrong? Did Peter get sent by mistake, instead of me?

Then I realized what had happened. Three weeks later in time Peter might be somewhere else. No wonder I couldn't see him.

There was no time to be lost. Rushing out of Peter's garage, I ran over to our house and entered through the back door.

Mother was in the kitchen. When she saw me, she stared. "Angela! I thought you were upstairs taking a shower!"

"Sorry!" I panted. "No time to talk!"

I dashed up to my room. Then I suddenly had a strange idea. What if I met *myself* in my room? Argh! It was a spooky thought.

There was nobody in my room. Where was I? I mean, where was the I of three weeks later?

Wait. Mother had just said she thought I was taking a shower. Down the hall, I could hear the water running in the bathroom. Okay. That meant I wouldn't run into me for a while.

I went to the shelf above my desk and frantically pawed

through the junk piled there. I found it! I found the latest issue of the school magazine, the one with the winning stories printed in it.

How much time had passed? Better hurry.

The shower had stopped running. This meant the other me was out of the bathroom. Have to get out of here!

Too late. Just as I started down the stairs, I heard Mother talking again. "Angela! A minute ago you were all dressed! Now you're in your robe again and your hair's all wet! I don't understand."

I shivered. It was scary, listening to Mother talking to myself downstairs. I heard my other self answering something, then the sound of her—my—steps coming up the stairs. In a panic, I dodged into the spare room and closed the door.

I heard the steps—my steps—go past and into my room.

The minute I heard the door of my room close, I rushed out and down the stairs.

Mother was standing at the foot of the stairs. When she saw me, her mouth dropped. "But . . . but . . . just a minute ago you were in your robe and your hair was all wet!"

"See you later, Mother," I panted. And I ran.

Behind me I heard Mother muttering, "I'm going mad!"

I didn't stop and try to explain. I might go mad, too.

It would be great if I could just keep the magazine with me. But, like the spring roll, it would get carried back to its own time after a few minutes. So the next best thing was to read the magazine as fast as I could.

It was hard to run and flip through the magazine at the same time. But I made it back to Peter's garage and plopped down on the stool.

At last I found the story: the story that had won the contest in our grade. I started to read.

Suddenly I heard *bleep, cheep,* and *gurgle,* and Peter loomed up in front of me. I was back in my original time again.

But I still had the magazine! Now I had to read the story before the magazine popped back to the future. It was hard to concentrate with Peter jumping up and down impatiently, so different from his usual calm, collected self.

I read a few paragraphs, and I was beginning to see how the story would shape up. But before I got any further, the magazine disappeared from my hand.

So I didn't finish reading the story. I didn't reach the end, where the name of the winning writer was printed.

That night I stayed up very late to write down what I remembered of the story. It had a neat plot, and I could see why it was the winner.

I hadn't read the entire story, so I had to make up the ending myself. But that was okay, since I knew how it should come out.

The winners of the writing contest would be announced at the school assembly on Friday. After we had filed into the assembly hall and sat down, the principal gave a speech. I tried not to fidget while he explained about the contest.

Suddenly I was struck by a dreadful thought. Somebody in my class had written the winning story, the one I had copied. Wouldn't that person be declared the winner, instead of me?

The principal started announcing the winners. I chewed my knuckles in an agony of suspense, as I waited to see who would be announced as the winner in my class. Slowly, the principal began with the lowest grade. Each winner walked in slow motion to the stage, while the principal slowly explained why the story was good.

At last, at last, he came to our grade. "The winner is . . ." He stopped, slowly got out his handkerchief, and slowly blew his nose. Then he cleared his throat. "The winning story is 'Around and Around,' by Angela Tang."

I sat like a stone, unable to move. Peter nudged me. "Go on, Angela! They're waiting for you."

I got up and walked up to the stage in a daze. The principal's voice seemed to be coming from far, far away as he told the audience that I had written a science fiction story about time travel.

The winners each got a notebook bound in imitation leather for writing more stories. Inside the cover of the notebook was a ballpoint pen. But the best prize was having my story in the school magazine with my name printed at the end.

Then why didn't I feel good about winning?

After assembly, the kids in our class crowded around to congratulate me. Peter formally shook my hand. "Good work, Angela," he said, and winked at me.

That didn't make me feel any better. I hadn't won the contest fairly. Instead of writing the story myself, I had copied it from the school magazine.

That meant someone in our class—one of the kids here—had

actually written the story. Who was it?

My heart was knocking against my ribs as I stood there and waited for someone to complain that I had stolen his story.

Nobody did.

As we were riding the school bus home, Peter looked at me. "You don't seem very happy about winning the contest, Angela."

"No, I'm not," I mumbled. "I feel just awful."

"Tell you what," suggested Peter. "Come over to my house and we'll discuss it."

"What is there to discuss?" I asked glumly. "I won the contest because I cheated."

"Come on over, anyway. My mother bought a fresh package of humbow in Chinatown."

I couldn't turn down that invitation. Humbow, a roll stuffed with barbecue pork, is my favorite snack.

Peter's mother came into the kitchen while we were munching, and he told her about the contest.

Mrs. Lu looked pleased. "I'm very glad, Angela. You have a terrific imagination, and you deserve to win."

"I like Angela's stories," said Peter. "They're original."

It was the first compliment he had ever paid me, and I felt my face turning red.

After Mrs. Lu left us, Peter and I each had another humbow. But I was still miserable. "I wish I had never started this. I feel like such a jerk."

Peter looked at me, and I swear he was enjoying himself. "If you stole another student's story, why didn't that person complain?"

"I don't know!" I wailed.

"Think!" said Peter. "You're smart, Angela. Come on, figure it out."

Me, smart? I was so overcome to hear myself called smart by a genius like Peter that I just stared at him.

He had to repeat himself. "Figure it out, Angela!"

I tried to concentrate. Why was Peter looking so amused?

The light finally dawned. "Got it," I said slowly. "*I'm* the one who wrote the story."

"The winning story is your own, Angela, because that's the one that won."

My head began to go around and around. "But where did the original idea for the story come from?"

"What made the plot so good?" asked Peter. His voice sounded unsteady.

"Well, in my story, my character used a time machine to go forward in time . . ."

"Okay, whose idea was it to use a time machine?"

"It was mine," I said slowly. I remembered the moment when the idea had hit me with a *boing*.

"So you s-stole f-from yourself!" sputtered Peter. He started to roar with laughter. I had never seen him break down like that. At this rate, he might wind up being human.

When he could talk again, he asked me to read my story to him.

I began. "'In movies, geniuses have frizzy white hair, right? They wear thick glasses and have names like Dr. Zweistein. . . .'"

The Piece of Straw

Yoshiko Uchida

A Folk Tale From Japan

LONG ago, in the land of Yamato, there was a poor young man who lived all alone. He had no family to care for him, and no friends to whom he could go for help. Each day he watched his purse grow slimmer and slimmer, for there was no one who would give him work. Finally, one day, he saw that his money was almost gone.

"Alas, what am I to do?" he sighed. "The only one who can help me now is the goddess of mercy at the Hase Temple."

So the poor young man hurried to the temple and knelt before the shrine of the goddess of mercy.

"Oh, Kannon-Sama," he said. "I am without food or money, and I cannot find work to keep myself alive. I shall kneel here before your shrine until you show me some way in which I can save myself."

The young man sat very still and waited for some sign from the goddess of mercy. "Show me in a dream just what I am to do," he pleaded. And the young man did not move from his place before the shrine. He sat there through the long night and all the next day, and still he had no dream. He sat there for many more days and nights, but still the goddess did not help him.

At last the priests of the temple noticed the young man who neither ate nor slept, but sat quietly in front of the shrine. "He will surely starve to death if he stays there much longer," they said to each other.

Then one of the priests went to question the young man.

"Who are you, my good fellow?" he asked. "And why do you sit here for so many days and nights?"

"Alas, I have no friend or family," said the young man sadly. "And since no one will give me work, I am almost without food or money. I have come here to ask the help of the goddess of mercy, but if she does not help me soon, I know that I shall die here before her shrine."

Now the good priests of the temple felt great pity for the poor young man and decided they would take turns bringing him food and water so he would not starve to death. So with their help, the young man continued to sit before the shrine for many more days and nights. He was growing sad and weary, and began to think perhaps the kind goddess would not help him after all.

At last, on the twenty-first day, as his head nodded with weariness and sleep, he thought he saw a faint dream. An old, old man with a flowing beard seemed to be coming out of the goddess's shrine. The old man stood before him and told him to leave the temple quickly. "The very first thing that your hand touches after you leave the temple will bring you much good fortune," the old man said to him. "So keep safely whatever it is, no matter how small it may be." And then the old man faded away just as quickly as he had appeared. The young man rubbed his eyes and looked around. The goddess of mercy was smiling down at him, just as she had for the last twenty-one days.

"Ah, that dream was her message to me," thought the young man, and he quickly prepared to leave the temple. The priests gave him some food to take along, and the young man hurried out through the temple gates. Just as he was about to turn onto the road, he tripped over a stone and fell flat on the dirt road. As he hastened to pick himself up, he saw that he was grasping a single piece of straw in his right hand. He started to throw it away, but he suddenly remembered what the old man had said to him: "The very first thing that your hand touches after you leave the temple will bring you much good fortune."

"But surely this little piece of straw can bring me no great fortune," thought the young man, and he was about to toss it on the roadside. Then he thought again, "No, I had better do exactly as the Kannon-Sama instructed me," so he carried the piece of straw carefully in his hand.

As he walked along the road, a horsefly began to buzz about his head. The young man picked up a stick and tried to shoo the fly away, but it would not stop bothering him. It buzzed and it buzzed, and it flew in little circles about his head. Finally the young man could bear it no longer. He cupped his hand, and with one big swoop, he caught the little horsefly. Then he strung it on the end of his stick with his piece of straw and walked on.

Before long, a carriage carrying a noblewoman and her son to the temple came rolling toward him. The little boy was weary and hot and was tired of sitting quietly in his carriage. He was fretting and crying, but he spied the horsefly buzzing on the end of the young man's stick.

"I want the little fly that's buzzing on the stick!" the little boy cried to his servant.

The servant approached the young man and said politely, "I wonder if you would be kind enough to give your stick to the little boy? He has grown weary from the long, hot ride, and this would make him very happy."

"Well, the fly is tied to the stick with a piece of straw which the goddess of the temple told me I must keep, but if it will make the little boy happy, I shall give it to him," said the young man.

"How very, very kind of you," the noblewoman said, as she leaned out of the carriage. "I'm afraid I have nothing with which I can repay you, except these three oranges." And she held out three large oranges on a beautiful white napkin.

The young man thanked the noblewoman, wrapped up the three oranges carefully, and walked down the road. The sun was hot as it beat down on the dusty road. Before long, he saw a procession of men and women coming toward him. They were walking on either side of a beautiful carriage, and appeared to be the handmaidens and guards of the noblewoman inside. As the group walked by the young man, one of the young women suddenly grew faint and collapsed at the side of the road.

"Oh, I am so thirsty," she said weakly, and held her hand out for some water.

"Quickly, find some water," the guards shouted, but there was no water to be seen anywhere.

They called to the young man and asked if he could tell them where there might be some water.

"I fear there are no wells or streams nearby," said the young man. "But I have three oranges here. Give her the juice from these oranges to quench her thirst," and he handed his oranges to the guards. They quickly gave the young maiden the juice from the three oranges, and before long she felt well enough to go on.

"If you had not come by and given me your oranges, I might have died here on this hot and dusty road," the maiden said to the young man. "I would give you anything to thank you, but I have only these three rolls of white silk. Take them and accept my thanks," she said, as she gave the rolls of silk to the young man.

The young man thanked her for the gift, and with the rolls of silk under his arm, he walked on down the road. "My goodness, one piece of straw brought me three oranges, and now my oranges have brought me three rolls of silk," thought the young man happily.

That night he found an inn where he could spend the night, and he gave the innkeeper one of the rolls of silk to pay for his room. Early the next morning, he started off down the road again. Toward noon, he saw a group of men on horseback cantering toward him. The horses held their heads up proudly, and whisked their long, shiny tails. The young man thought he had never seen such beautiful horses before, and looked at them longingly, for he had always wanted a horse for himself. Then, just as one of the noblemen rode past the young man, his horse suddenly faltered and fell to the ground. The men gathered about the animal and stroked its side and gave it water, but the horse would not move or raise its head.

"I'm afraid it's dead," said the nobleman sadly, and he took the saddle from the horse's back and the bit from its mouth. He then left one of his servants to care for the horse's remains, and rode off on another horse with his men.

The young man went up to the servant who was left to care for the horse. "He must have been a very fine horse," said the young man, as he looked down at the dead animal.

"Oh, yes, indeed he was," answered the servant. "He was such a valuable animal that even though many people offered large sums of money, the master would not think of selling him. It certainly is strange that he died so suddenly," he added, shaking his head.

"What are you going to do now?" the young man asked.

"I can't let the horse just lie here beside the road. I really don't know what to do," answered the servant sadly.

"Well, if you like, I'll give you a roll of silk for the horse. Then you can return home, and I shall take care of the horse," said the young man.

"What a strange person to want a dead horse," thought the servant. "Why, that is a fine bargain, my friend," he said out loud, and he quickly took the roll of silk and hurried away before the young man should change his mind.

The young man knelt down before the horse and prayed to the goddess of mercy that he might come to life again. "Oh, Kannon-Sama," he pleaded, "please give life to this beautiful horse once more." Then, as he watched, the horse slowly opened its eyes. Then it slowly got to its feet, and before long, began to drink water and eat some oats. It shook its head, whisked its long, silky tail, and looked as good as new once again. The young man was so happy he quickly climbed up on the horse's back and rode into the next village. There he spent the night at another inn and used his last roll of silk to pay for his room.

The next day, he rode on his fine horse until he came to the town of Toba. He knew he wasn't far from the big city of Kyoto, when, suddenly, the young man thought of a problem. The nobleman was very well known in Kyoto and many people probably knew his beautiful chestnut-colored horse. "It would never do if I should be accused of stealing the nobleman's horse," he thought, "for no one would believe the strange story of how the horse came to be mine."

So the young man decided he would sell the horse. Just then, he passed by the home of a family who appeared to be getting ready to leave on a journey. A wagon piled high with bags and boxes stood by the front gate. The young man called out to the man of the house, "Good sir, would you like to buy this horse from me?"

"My, what a beautiful horse. I certainly would like to buy it from you, but alas, I have no money," he answered.

Then the man came closer to look at the horse. It was more beautiful than any he had ever seen.

"Ah, what a pity I cannot buy such a fine animal," he said. "But wait, I know what I can do. I can give you three rice fields in exchange for your horse," said the man happily.

The young man thought for a moment. "Well—" he began.

"What's more, since we are going away, I shall leave you the house, and you may live in it until we return," continued the man.

"That's a fair bargain indeed," said the young man. "The horse is yours!"

"In case we decide not to return, the house will be yours too," called the man, and soon he and his family rode off down the road with their wagon rumbling after them.

Now the young man found that one field of rice was plenty to keep him well fed, so he rented out his other fields. As if by magic, the rice in his field grew and grew, until he had so much rice, he could sell many, many sacks each day. He grew richer and richer, and his purse grew fatter and fatter, and his luck seemed to grow with the years.

Many years went by, and still no one returned to the house,

so the young man continued to live there and raise fine crops of rice. His wealth increased tenfold, and he became an important man in the town. He married a beautiful young maiden of the village, and they had many lovely children. And there they lived happily for many years with their children and with their children's children in the town of Toba.

So the one little piece of straw which the young man picked up so many years ago outside the temple gate had truly brought him great good fortune and happiness, just as the old man in his dream had said it would.

from
Baba

Belle Yang

Weather Reports

A dab of cloud scuttled across the unblemished sky like a white mouse.

"What do you think? A rain cloud? You think it might rain?" Baba heard folk ask one another as they rubbed their chins and scratched their heads. They searched their neighbors' faces for a confirmation of the hope.

In Baba's thirteenth summer, the sorghum reached only the height of a man's shoulders and withered.

Sorghum was the staple of the North. Now all that was left to eat was a heavy, coarse meal—a mixture of corn and soybean.

As a precautionary measure, children were not allowed more than a bowl and a half of the stuff, for it ballooned inside the stomach after fluids were taken; and since folk were likely to drink a lot of water after eating the salty, fermented bean sauce that was the ubiquitous accompaniment to northern meals, gluttony was especially dangerous; it was rumored that some had burst their stomachs and died in great agony.

The following spring, the sky again promised to be tightfisted: it was the second year into the drought.

"Last year, the Almanac said there were to be nine dragons spouting water. Should have been a decent year for rain, but there was hardly a drop," said Nainai, my grandmother, with a sniff of disgust.

She consulted the Imperial Almanac. Each yearly issue gave a forecast of the amount of rain that would fall upon the land and offered other vital information, such as favorable days for births and marriages, appropriate days for funerals, safe days for journeys, lucky days for raising roof beams and moving furniture. The Almanac was all that one needed to negotiate the uncertainties of life.

"This year, it says there are to be twelve dragons in the sky. Aiya, really terrible . . . twelve lazy dragons!" said Nainai.

"But, Mother, doesn't more dragons mean more rain?" asked Baba.

"No, of course not. Remember the adage about the monks?"
Baba shook his head.

"'One thirsty monk will use a shoulder pole to carry two
buckets of water; two thirsty monks will shoulder only one
bucket of water on a pole between them; three thirsty monks
will remain three thirsty monks.'

"This is also the way of the dragons: the more dragons there
are for rainmaking, the more each will shuck his share of the
work."

April brought no rain. May brought no rain. The men and
women of Xinmin looked up at the azure sky through eyes slot-
ted by doubt and fear. The sun buckled the earth, shaking dust
into the air.

"If there's no rain this year, we won't even have the early-
season crops of soybean and corn. Everyone's sick of the stuff—
just the smell of it makes me ill—but it is better than the thin,
dry odor of hunger," the people said. Their stomachs anticipated
the grinding of emptiness; hunger was an inherited remembrance.

"We must pray to Dragon King for rain," the elders advised.
"We have neglected him for too long." Ancient prayers were
dusted off in their memories.

Dragon King, the severe but reasonable ruler of the oceans
and rivers, the great creator of the Yellow River—the cradle of
Chinese civilization. Dragon King, the source of life.

On a June morning, a day decreed by the mayor of Xinmin,
business owners and residents along the main thoroughfares
burned incense upon outdoor tables set up to honor the god.
Flowing calligraphy on vermilion paper posted upon the walls
above the tables read: "Dragon King, the rainmaker, the ruler of
the five lakes, four oceans, nine rivers, and eight streams, is en-
throned among us."

On this appointed day, each family was required to send one
male representative to the site of the largest well in the city,
there to join the multitude in paying homage to the heavenly
rainmaker. Baba eagerly volunteered to represent the House of
Yang; permission was quickly granted, as no one else had a
midge of desire for the job.

Baba arrived at the site clad only in shorts; upon his head
rested a crown of braided willow; the tender green shoots feath-
ering down to his shoulders provided scant protection from the
sun. Similarly outfitted were all the men and boys who sought
audience with Dragon King.

A table set against the well displayed candles and incense, and these were lit as the mayor read a prayer to Dragon King that had been written in vermilion ink upon a sheet of yellow paper:

"We have come before you, O Dragon King, to make an entreaty to your generous soul: O bringer of life, grace our land with rain, for without water to our fields, we will have nothing for the winter stores.

"If you should grant us rain this summer, O Lord, we the folk of Xinmin will dedicate ourselves to raising a glorious new temple in your honor."

Baba thought: It's just like what Mama says to bribe my little sister when she's a nuisance: "If you are a good girl, come New Year, Mother will make you a pretty little jacket to wear."

A modest temple to Dragon King was already in existence on the outskirts of Xinmin, along the bank of the river Liu. It had been forgotten during the years of good rains; the fiery red of the temple pillars had long been extinguished and had turned a powdery pink, but no one thought to repaint them. No one came to make offerings; the local incense business trickled down to nothing. Now that the people needed help from Dragon King, they could not do enough to accommodate him. The incense business picked up considerably.

After the prayer, the mayor burned the yellow paper and kowtowed at the mouth of the well. The gathering, following his movements, bowed in silence.

As the kneeling men and boys covered the ground like thousands of ripened melons in a patch, fifteen monstrous red drums, each carried by two men, and fifteen sets of cymbals entered the scene, to boom and crash a reminder to Dragon King: "Lest you've forgotten, O Great One, this is what the sound of rainmaking is like."

Water from the well, flung from buckets, doused the grateful men and boys. Another reminder: "Lest you forget, O Dragon King, this is what rain looks like."

Afterward, following the lead of the mayor and other dignitaries, the crowd wended its way across town, itself looking like the long, thrashing tail of a dragon.

The persistent *doong-doong-doong-doong!* of the drums troubled the earth; the heavy pulse invaded Baba's soul through the bottoms of his bare, marching feet. The cymbals clamored like ten thousand angry wives flinging washbasins, the vibrations rattling the desiccated leaves upon treetops and clattering the bowls in the cupboards.

The Japanese vice mayor, among the handful of Japanese officials in attendance, was the most devout of the supplicants, displaying an unparalleled zeal. (The Japanese had been in Manchuria for nearly a decade but, on the whole, were unobtrusive; they held subordinate titles such as Vice Mayor, Assistant Superintendent of Schools, or Deputy Chief of Police, but de facto power was in their hands. Most folk had little or no direct dealings with them. Schoolchildren, however, were given their daily doses of Japanese-language lessons by stern Japanese teachers.) The vice mayor, overpowered by primal music, danced and weaved like a drunkard through the streets.

Women along the parade route readied tubs of water to shower upon the procession.

By the end of the afternoon, all the larger wells in Xinmin had been visited with prayers. The people dispersed. Baba returned home, limp, dusty, and cooked as pink as shrimp.

Sure enough, three days after the ceremony, the sky came to boil with black clouds. Lightning! and then *gooloong, gooloong, goolooloooloong!* sounded high above. The dragons were at work, threading through the thunderheads that had conspired farther north.

The rain came down. Not tickling rain, as fine as the hair on the nape of a cow: that kind foretold only more of the same. No, it was a steady downpour, which fingered through the soil, deeply massaging the earth. Ah, the smell of rain! Dragon King had heard their entreaties.

Baba watched the sorghum grow to its full height that season; the tassels of the ripened grain turned russet—a red to warm men's hearts.

The people of Xinmin kept their promise: by fall, work had begun on the new temple, upon the site of the old.

Throughout the numbing winter, carpenters labored to carve symbols of good omen upon the beams and latticework; craftsmen molded statues of gods and spirits from clay; artists breathed upon their brushes to keep the pigments from freezing upon the hairs as they painted murals.

On an April day, Baba joined the hordes at the opening ceremony. Vendors hawked live ducks and geese, pinwheels made from bamboo, and candied haws, which children clamored for. A temporary stage was erected, upon which opera singers contributed their share to the general cacophony.

Baba was eager to meet Dragon King. He squeezed into the temple, which smelled wonderfully of fresh paint and lacquer. In the temple hall he was hailed by a figure with the head of a dragon—a furry mustache under a bulbous red nose, protruding eyes, sharp teeth, and antlers—and the body of a human being, who, standing arms akimbo, wore the long yellow robe of an emperor. When he could get close enough, Baba ran his fingers over the carved folds of the robe.

To either side of the god were his lieutenants: unsavory-looking characters with heads of fish, turtle, crab, and prawn. Behind them spread the deep green bottom of the sea, brimming with creatures that swam between the columns of the god's shimmering crystal palace. Baba's head was made dizzy by the splendor of the artists' imaginings.

The ensuing summer was also a season of plentiful rain; the tassels on the sorghum had grown a foot long. But just before the harvest, suddenly, the rivers Liu and Liao, converging just south of Xinmin, swelled and overflowed their banks. Rainfall had been normal in Xinmin, but there had been torrential rains to the northwest, in the direction of Inner Mongolia. The water surged over the banks and drowned the fields, leaving only the tassels of the sorghum to thrash about above the bull-roaring, murky water.

"How did we come to deserve this?" the people asked. "We've broken our backs to build a temple in honor of Dragon King, yet the water still works against us."

Seers (the only beneficiaries of crises and tears) were consulted.

One said: "You have forgotten about the very powerful Catfish Demon. His magic has grown to fearsome proportions, for he has spent the last two thousand years in meditation. You have aroused his jealously by all the fuss over Dragon King and his attendant spirits. Now this demon of the rivers is throwing a tantrum. A temple must be built in his honor if you want to soothe and smooth down the waters."

Baba attended the noisy grand opening of the temple to the Catfish Demon and gazed in awe upon the exquisite ugliness of the god's liver-colored, bewhiskered face.

In the following year, the rivers were well behaved and the sky accommodating. And as before, the incense business went into decline.

● ● ●

Fire Wagons

My father's third grandaunt had only heard about fire wagons. She had never seen one. The north-south railroad line running from Shenyang to Beiping had been in existence for decades, but it did not rumble through her village.

"Fire wagons . . . fire wagons," Baba heard her say at the House of Yang. "How queer for a wagon to run on flames." She knew wheelbarrows, cow wagons, donkey carts, and horse carts, but a fire wagon was something beyond the bubble of her world and imagination.

She had never ventured outside her native village of Shantuozi. When she came to Xinmin to attend the big white celebration, the funeral ceremony of her clansman, it was the first time she had traveled the sixty li—a day's journey by wagon—to the neighboring city.

Women—and especially country women like her—had few opportunities for adventure, however mild: they were made busy holding up more than their half of the world.

As girls, they were kept within the narrow confines of their homes, feeding the geese, goats, pigs, and chickens; sewing clothes; embroidering; making shoes. It was improper for unmarried young women to be perused by strangers on the streets.

As they grew older, opportunities to venture out came even more rarely, for after they married, their time was taken up entirely by cooking, washing, waiting on the husbands and the in-laws, and raising the bumper crops of children. Only when they reached old age, when they had daughters-in-law themselves to do the tedious chores, did they merit attendance at weddings and funerals of relatives in distant places.

Third Grandauntie was short and plump and walked with the curious hip sway of women with miniaturized feet (they were liberated from the bandages used for foot-binding when she was already an adult). Baba always heard her laughing and giggling, for as a matriarch of nearly seventy with a troop of daughters-in-law (and an army of grandchildren), she had little to worry her soul.

"Third Grandauntie, if you'd like, I can take you to the station to see the fire wagons for yourself," Baba heard Second Brother say.

Elder Brother, standing next to Baba, groaned. He considered himself a scholar and had no time for such nonsense.

Nainai shot a worried look in her second son's direction, as she puffed silently on her long-stemmed pipe.

"Take me along too! I've never seen a fire wagon either," said a bent old matron from the country.

"Nor I," echoed another.

Only Second Brother, his soul as deep and wide as the Yellow Sea, would think to play tour guide to gammers from the countryside. He was an athletic, companionable fellow; a man with a toothy grin and lots of laughter. Everyone liked him.

They began their outing at eight o'clock the following morning. Second Brother, like a hefty mother hen, had half a dozen cheerful, chirping ladies—hair up in slicked-back, neat little buns—trailing him to the train station across town.

They arrived with only a few minutes to spare. The once-a-day southbound train from Shenyang "galloped and reared in, belching smoke," as Third Grandauntie described it.

"I'll buy everyone a platform ticket. Then all you ladies can get a closer look," said Second Brother. "It'll be much better than craning your necks from this waiting room window."

The train slowed to a stop.

"Aiyaya! *Mrrr, mrrr, mrrr*—it cries as loud as ten cows, but it is ten thousand times bigger," said Grandauntie as she gazed upon the beast, her toothless mouth sprung open.

"They've come so far . . . why not let them have a look inside," said Second Brother to himself. He boosted his brood, one by one, into the nearest passenger car.

"Hai, how elegant! How lovely!" They sighed and twittered. They ran their hands along the backs of the shiny black vinyl seats, touched the starched green tablecloths, and fingered the porcelain vases adorned with silk flowers. It was like nothing they'd ever seen back home.

As Second Brother tried to school them toward the rear exit, the train began to pull out of the station.

"Hurry! Hurry! Please go quickly! We must get off!" he cried; but his charges, twisting and swiveling on their tiny feet, could not shift any faster.

"Aiya! We're moving," said one delighted grandma.

"Yes, sister, we most certainly are. There's no lurching at all—the ride is smoother than the horse carts with the newfangled rubber tires," said Third Grandauntie.

Second Brother was sweating like a rain cloud. "I only paid for platform tickets. Now I've no more money, and we're on our way to Beiping. . . . What am I going to tell the folks back home? . . . If we ever manage to get back home."

"This is strange. Number Two Son has been gone with the womenfolk since morning," said Yeye at the House of Yang.

Baba saw that his father's face was ashen. "We sent Number Four and the wagoner to bring them all home, but they were not to be found. There was no sign of them anywhere. How could that be? It isn't as if we're searching for one lost needle." Yeye liked life orderly and without surprises.

"Only Number Two would be softheaded enough to take them. Only he could manage to lose them all—and himself in the bargain," Eldest Brother said with a sneer.

"I was afraid something just like this would occur," said Nainai. "Aiya, to have a worrisome son like this Number Two. On the day I was born, hail the size of duck eggs descended from the sky; this, the seers said to my mother, would mean that I would be living life as a series of unfolding disasters. Hunnh, how right they were. Why, it was just last winter that Number Two—that bad egg—brought me so much trouble. Do you all remember what happened?!"

How could Baba forget? Rarely had he seen his mother so angry.

His second, and favorite, of four brothers, older by six years, loved food. Good food. Once he was old enough to hold a job, he went to work as an accountant for Xinmin County. He could then afford to leave behind the jostling dinner table, the dueling chopsticks, and the unappealing food cooked in bulk to feed a large family.

Nattily attired in a Western suit and sporting a tweed cap, he frequented the restaurants that catered mouthwatering delicacies such as "lion's head," "pork potstickers with silver ears," and "mutton hot pot."

Baba was envious of his brother, for he was still young and had to eat at home. In the winter, when he helped his brother on with his heavy winter coat, he was allowed to fish in the pocket for loose coins with which to buy morsels of roasted donkey meat; the sinewy flesh above the hoof of the unfortunate beast was all he could afford. But more often, he shadowed Second Brother to the restaurants, to be fed for the price of not tattling on the elder's indulgence.

The previous year, his brother had outspent his meager income but continued to patronize his favorite eateries, charging the bills to the county government.

Of course, the county would not pay for his excess. At the end of the year, when all obligations had to be met, he was faced with the prospect of spending Spring Festival, the Chinese New Year, in debtors' prison.

"Wife, how will we pay the bill for Number Two's big appetite? I have no income of my own," Yeye had said to Nainai. "Now you must return to your mother's house and sell your cattle. How else to rescue him? We cannot ask the Patriarch for the money, for the other family members will surely look on red-eyed and make a big fuss. Ah, you must go quickly, to save the face of the House of Yang."

When Nainai was a girl, she had earned money by gleaning the soybean fields after harvest. She had saved to buy a cow; later on, when she had more money, she bought the solitary cow a mate. Not surprisingly, left to themselves, the animals reproduced.

Nainai's nephew had been charged with the care of the herd when she married.

Over the busy years, as a daughter-in-law whose days revolved around the hot kitchen stove at the House of Yang, she thought of her cattle only rarely, but now, confronted with selling them, Nainai was reminded of how hard she had worked as a girl to acquire them; it did not please her in the least to sacrifice her animals to save her spendthrift son.

Nainai traveled in the back of a mule-drawn wagon in the snow for the two-day journey to her mother's house in the country; there she compelled her nephew to drive five head of cattle to market.

The nephew did so with great reluctance, for since her marriage, his aunt had never made mention of her property; he had been hoping that she had forgotten about them entirely. Besides, her cattle had bred with his and multiplied, and now no one had a clear account of which animals belonged to whom.

"Since the sale had to take place in such a big hurry," the nephew said to Nainai, "I was only able to sell two cattle out of the five." (Perhaps, at market, he had simply decided to part with only two.)

"And they sold at a very bad price," the nephew added. (Perhaps, at home, he had simply decided to hand over the money for only one.)

"Never mind," Nainai said when she heard the bad news. "I must get back to Xinmin quickly."

She returned, braving the snow, just in the nick of time to save Baba's second brother from the jailer.

The winter sun slid rapidly down into the west as the family waited and waited with mounting alarm and anger, imagining all sorts of tragic ends.

When, finally, Baba was pressed once again to search at the train station, he heard the dogs barking at the gate and peals of laughter just outside.

"I'm so hungry, I can eat an entire roast pig by myself," came the voice of Third Grandauntie, who was leading the pack of tired but happy women warriors; not a single strand of her hair had come loose from her tight little bun.

"We went all the way to Willow Creek Village! In less than half an hour, we traveled twenty-five li!" explained Grandauntie to Baba between giggles. "We had to wait the entire afternoon to return on another fire wagon. We had no money for the tickets . . . but Number Two convinced them that the House of Yang would most certainly take care of the bill later."

Second Brother, who was bringing up the rear, smiled sheepishly.

"Out the windows, I saw the trees and poles, the mules and dogs, run backward!" continued my father's third Grandauntie. "Can you imagine that . . . can you just imagine! The world goes by different rules outside of my home in Shantuozi."

Forbidden Fruit

Paul Yee

MANY years ago, in a valley deep in the heart of the New World, the farmer, Fong, cleared the forest and staked out his land. Day after day he pushed a wooden plough through the unbroken soil and drew long dark lines to the hazy horizon.

Through the long hot summers Farmer Fong watered his crops; through the deep dark winters he built up his barn. Working the soil nourished his soul just as the food he grew nourished his body. How he smiled when the sunshine soaked his back, or when rain filled the furrows in his field.

Farmer Fong smiled also at the thought of his three sons and one daughter. Their mother had died giving birth to the baby sister, but she was loved the best. The three boys made sure that her farm chores were never too heavy, and they helped her in the kitchen. Farmer Fong watched his children grow into fine adults, and he dreamed of how his farm would expand and prosper.

But the three boys did not stay. Their ears perked to the tales of travelers, and their eyes followed horses headed for far-off places. Farmer Fong tried to make them see the magic of the soil that moved him, but the words did not come easily. One by one the sons went off. The eldest son strapped on a shoulder pack and panned for gold along the northern rivers. The second son seized a shovel and stoked coal inside steamships sailing along the rocky coast. The youngest hitched his saddle and worked on the wagon trains and stagecoaches.

Farmer Fong watched bitterly as his sons trekked away. He shouted after them, "If you leave now, you are no longer my sons! Never cross my gate again, never call me Father! You are all finished!"

He turned and hurled his fury at the daughter. He worked her in the fields like an ox, and he complained about her cooking at every meal. He stamped his boot on the floorboards to waken her in the mornings and cursed her mother for bearing such wayward boys. But the daughter understood his anger and let it flow by her.

One day a young man appeared at their door. He was covered

with dust. "I have walked many miles looking for work," he said. "I will work for you if you can give me shelter and three meals a day."

Farmer Fong looked the man over and nodded. The young man's hair was cropped short and bristled thick and full. Sweat and blowing dust had hardened his shirt and pants.

The daughter smiled at the man and rejoiced that someone had come to share her labor.

Through the long hot summer the daughter and the young man worked side by side. Together they pulled at weeds and pumped for water. They pedaled the waterwheel and made crates and sacks for packing. At harvest time, they spent weary weeks bent over the fields, hacking and pulling at the crops. They labored as equals and darkened under the sun.

And every evening after dinner, they sat on the verandah, rubbing their aching muscles and fanning themselves. The daughter wept softly, remembering her brothers, and the man held her in his arms. But nothing could be done.

One morning after the harvest, the farmhand put on a clean shirt and asked Farmer Fong if he could marry his daughter. Farmer Fong refused, saying his daughter could not marry a man without means. Without a word, the young man gathered his goods and departed. The daughter watched him leave just as her brothers had done before, and she felt a thin bolt of lightning lance her heart.

She crumpled onto the floor and was carried to bed where she lay with her eyes closed, scarcely breathing. Farmer Fong watched helplessly as his beloved daughter grew weaker, and his anger melted. He sent for ancient herbs, he sent for the doctor. But even the strongest medicines and richest broths could not restore her strength.

The doctor shook his head. "I can do nothing," he said. "It is not a sickness of the body."

Farmer Fong knelt by the bed and grasped his daughter's hand. "Tell me what makes you ill, daughter!" he cried. "Tell me what will set you well again!"

Her eyelids lifted and she whispered, "Bring me news of the one I love."

Farmer Fong swallowed hard. Then he sent urgent letters to his three sons. He told them of their sister's illness and described the farmhand. He ordered them to find him. "Please hurry!" he wrote.

Weeks passed. Then one day the eldest son strode in from the mountains. "Your loved one pans for gold by an icy stream," he reported. "He sends these tokens of his love."

He placed cool lumps of gold and jade into his sister's hands. But they fell from her fingers, because she knew her brother was lying.

Then the second brother came back from the ocean. "He has set up shop as a merchant in a port city," he told her. "He sends these gifts to speak his heart."

He unrolled bolts of soft silk and shiny brocade before her, but she knew his story was false, too.

Finally the youngest son galloped up on his horse. "He is fighting heaven and earth to reclaim new farmlands!" he cried. "He had nothing but these to send you."

He pressed some dry, wrinkled seeds into her hands. They softened at her touch and tiny tendrils began to sprout. The daughter felt life tingle warm inside her like the first sunshine of spring. Swiftly she set the seeds into pots by her window and watched them grow.

When the days grew mild enough, she planted the seedlings in the soil outside. Daily she tended the rows, feeding and speaking to the plants as if they were human. Farmer Fong smiled with relief as his daughter's health improved.

Then one night a cold spell seized the valley. The daughter rushed out to wrap cloth around her plants to keep the frost away, and Farmer Fong built a huge bonfire to warm the seedlings. But icy winds swept the fire out and blew the heat away. The little plants froze and shriveled. The daughter fell to the ground weeping and, in the arms of her sorrowing father, she soon died.

After she was buried, Farmer Fong found a small pot of seeds left in his daughter's room. He planted these with great care. When the seedlings came up, he propped panes of glass around them to protect them from the cold.

The plants sprang up tall and strong. Fruit appeared on the branches and slowly ripened into a deep blood-red. And when Farmer Fong bit into the fruit, the juices gushed sharp and sweet, reminding him of his daughter's gentle nature and his own foolish pride.

From then on, Farmer Fong continued to grow the plants. He built walls and ceilings of glass to enclose the long rows of seedlings. In these greenhouses, the tomatoes flourished and were shipped to all parts of the country. The brother on the wagon trail heaved crates of them. The sailor brother delivered them to farflung coastal towns, and the miner found them on his plate when he came to town for a meal. They sniffed at the fruit's fragrance, stared at its glossy red and hefted its soft firmness in their dark strong hands. Thus they were always reminded of their sister and her love for the farmhand Johnson.

You're Short, Besides!

Sucheng Chan

Originally appeared in *Making Waves: An Anthology of Writings by and about Asian American Women,* edited by Asian Women United of California, copyright Sucheng Chan.

WHEN asked to write about being a physically handicapped Asian-American woman, I considered it an insult. After all, my accomplishments are many, yet I was not asked to write about any of them. Is being handicapped the most salient feature about me? The fact that it might be in the eyes of others made me decide to write the essay as requested. I realized that the way I think about myself may differ considerably from the way others perceive me. And maybe that's what being physically handicapped is all about.

I was stricken simultaneously with pneumonia and polio at the age of four. Uncertain whether I had polio of the lungs, seven of the eight doctors who attended me—all practitioners of Western medicine—told my parents they should not feel optimistic about my survival. A Chinese fortuneteller my mother consulted also gave a grim prognosis, but for an entirely different reason: I had been stricken because my name was offensive to the gods. My grandmother had named me "grandchild of wisdom," a name that the fortuneteller said was too presumptuous for a girl. So he advised my parents to change my name to "chaste virgin." All these pessimistic predictions notwithstanding, I hung onto life, if only by a thread. For three years, my body was periodically pierced with electric shocks as the muscles of my legs atrophied. Before my illness, I had been an active, rambunctious, precocious, and very curious child. Being confined to bed was thus a mental agony as great as my physical pain. Living in war-torn China, I received little medical attention; physical therapy was unheard of. But I was determined to walk. So one day, when I was six or seven, I instructed my mother to set up two rows of chairs to face each other so that I could use them as I would parallel bars. I attempted to walk by holding my body up and moving it forward with my arms while dragging my legs along behind. Each time I fell, my mother gasped, but I badgered her until she let me try again. After four nonambulatory years, I finally walked once more by pressing my hands against my thighs so my knees wouldn't buckle.

My father had been away from home during most of those years because of the war. When he returned, I had to confront the guilt he felt about my condition. In many East Asian cultures, there is a strong folk belief that a person's physical state in this life is a reflection of how morally or sinfully he or she lived in previous lives. Furthermore, because of the tendency to view the family as a single unit, it is believed that the fate of one member can be caused by the behavior of another. Some of my father's relatives told him my illness had doubtless been caused by the wild carousing he did in his youth. A well-meaning but somewhat simple man, my father believed them.

Throughout my childhood, he sometimes apologized to me for having to suffer retribution for his former bad behavior. This upset me; it was bad enough that I had to deal with the anguish of not being able to walk, but to have to assuage his guilt as well was a real burden! In other ways, my father was very good to me. He took me out often, carrying me on his shoulders or back, to give me fresh air and sunshine. He did this until I was too large and heavy for him to carry. And ever since I can remember, he has told me that I am pretty.

After getting over her anxieties about my constant falls, my mother decided to send me to school. I had already learned to read some words of Chinese at the age of three by asking my parents to teach me the sounds and meaning of various characters in the daily newspaper. But between the ages of four and eight, I received no education since just staying alive was a full-time job. Much to her chagrin, my mother found no school in Shanghai, where we lived at the time, which would accept me as a student. Finally, as a last resort, she approached the American School which agreed to enroll me only if my family kept an *amah* (a servant who takes care of children) by my side at all times. The tuition at the school was twenty U.S. dollars per month—a huge sum of money during those years of runaway inflation in China—and payable only in U.S. dollars. My family afforded the high cost of tuition and the expense of employing a full-time *amah* for less than a year.

We left China as the Communist forces swept across the country in victory. We found an apartment in Hong Kong across the street from a school run by Seventh-Day Adventists. By that time I could walk a little, so the principal was persuaded to accept me. An *amah* now had to take care of me only during recess when my classmates might easily knock me over as they ran about the playground.

After a year and a half in Hong Kong, we moved to Malaysia, where my father's family had lived for four generations. There I learned to swim in the lovely warm waters of the tropics and fell in love with the sea. On land I was a cripple; in the ocean I could move with the grace of a fish. I liked the freedom of being in the water so much that many years later, when I was a graduate student in Hawaii, I became greatly enamored with a man just because he called me a "Polynesian water nymph."

As my overall health improved, my mother became less anxious about all aspects of my life. She did everything possible to enable me to lead as normal a life as possible. I remember how once some of her colleagues in the high school where she taught criticized her for letting me wear short skirts. They felt my legs should not be exposed to public view. My mother's response was, "All girls her age wear short skirts, so why shouldn't she?"

The years in Malaysia were the happiest of my childhood, even though I was constantly fending off children who ran after me calling, *"Baikah! Baikah!"* ("Cripple! Cripple!" in the Hokkien dialect commonly spoken in Malaysia). The taunts of children mattered little because I was a star pupil. I won one award after another for general scholarship as well as for art and public speaking. Whenever the school had important visitors, my teacher always called on me to recite in front of the class.

A significant event that marked me indelibly occurred when I was twelve. That year my school held a music recital, and I was one of the students chosen to play the piano. I managed to get up the steps to the stage without any problem, but as I walked across the stage, I fell. Out of the audience, a voice said loudly and clearly, "Ayah! A *baikah* shouldn't be allowed to perform in public." I got up before anyone could get on stage to help me, and with tears streaming uncontrollably down my face, I rushed to the piano and began to play. Beethoven's "Für Elise" had never been played so fiendishly fast before or since, but I managed to finish the whole piece. That I managed to do so made me feel really strong. I never again feared ridicule.

In later years I was reminded of this experience from time to time. During my fourth year as an assistant professor at the University of California at Berkeley, I won a distinguished teaching award. Some weeks later I ran into a former professor who congratulated me enthusiastically. But I said to him, "You know what? I became a distinguished teacher by *limping* across the stage of Dwinelle 155!" (Dwinelle 155 is a large, cold classroom that most colleagues of mine hate to teach in.) I was rude not because I lacked graciousness but because this man, who had told me that my dissertation was the finest piece of work he had read in fifteen years, had nevertheless advised me to eschew a teaching career.

"Why?" I asked.

"Your leg . . ." he responded.

"What about my leg?" I said, puzzled.

"Well, how would you feel standing in front of a large lecture class?"

"If it makes any difference, I want you to know I've won a number of speech contests in my life, and I am not the least bit self-conscious about speaking in front of large audiences. . . . Look, why don't you write me a letter of recommendation to tell people how brilliant I am, and let *me* worry about my leg!"

This incident is worth recounting only because it illustrates a dilemma that handicapped persons face frequently: those who care about us sometimes get so protective that they unwittingly limit our growth. This former professor of mine had been one of my greatest supporters for two decades. Time after time, he had written glowing letters of recommendation on my behalf. He had spoken as he did because he thought he had my best interests at heart; he thought that if I got a desk job rather than one that required me to be a visible, public person, I would be spared the misery of being stared at.

Americans, for the most part, do not believe as Asians do that physically handicapped persons are morally flawed. But they are equally inept at interacting with those of us who are not able-bodied. Cultural differences in the perception and treatment of handicapped people are most clearly expressed by adults. Children, regardless of where they are, tend to be openly curious about people who do not look "normal." Adults in Asia have no hesitation in asking visibly handicapped people what is wrong with them, often expressing their sympathy with looks of pity, whereas adults in the United States try desperately to be polite by pretending not to notice.

One interesting response I often elicited from people in Asia but have never encountered in America is the attempt to link my physical condition to the state of my soul. Many a time while living and traveling in Asia people would ask me what religion I belonged to. I would tell them my mother is a devout Buddhist, that my father was baptized a Catholic but has never practiced Catholicism, and that I am an agnostic. Upon hearing this, people would try strenuously to convert me to their religion so that whichever God they believed in could bless me. If I would only attend this church or that temple regularly, they urged, I would surely get cured. Catholics and Buddhists alike have pressed religious medallions into my palm, telling me if I would wear these, the relevant deity or saint would make me well. Once while visiting the tomb of Muhammad Ali Jinnah in Karachi, Pakistan, an old Muslim, after finishing his evening prayers, spotted me, gestured toward my legs, raised his arms heavenward, and began a new round of prayers, apparently on my behalf.

In the United States adults who try to act "civilized" towards handicapped people by pretending they don't notice anything unusual sometimes end up ignoring handicapped people completely. In the first few months I lived in this country, I was struck by the fact that whenever children asked me what was the matter with my leg, their adult companions would hurriedly shush them up, furtively look at me, mumble apologies, and rush their children away. After a few months of such encounters, I decided it was my responsibility to educate these people. So I would say to the flustered adults, "It's okay; let the kid ask." Turning to the child, I would say, "When I was a little girl, no bigger than you are, I became sick with something called polio. The muscles of my leg shrank up, and I couldn't walk very well. You're much luckier than I am because now you can get a vaccine to make sure you never get my disease. So don't cry when your mommy takes you to get a polio vaccine, okay?" Some adults and their little companions I talked to this way were glad to be rescued from embarrassment; others thought I was strange.

Americans have another way of covering up their uneasiness: they become jovially patronizing. Sometimes when people spot my crutch, they ask if I've had a skiing accident. When I answer that unfortunately it is something less glamorous than that, they say, "I bet you *could* ski if you put your mind to it." Alternately, at parties where people dance, men who ask me to dance with them get almost belligerent when I decline their invitation. They say, "Of course you can dance if you *want* to!" Some have given me pep talks about how if I would only develop the right mental attitude, I would have more fun in life.

Different cultural attitudes toward handicapped persons came out clearly during my wedding. My father-in-law, as solid a representative of middle America as could be found, had no qualms about objecting to the marriage on racial grounds, but he could bring himself to comment on my handicap only indirectly. He wondered why his son, who had dated numerous high school and college beauty queens, couldn't marry one of them instead of me. My mother-in-law, a devout Christian, did not share her husband's prejudices, but she worried aloud about whether I could have children. Some Chinese friends of my parents, on the other hand, said that I was lucky to have found such a noble man, one who would marry me despite my handicap. I, for my part, appeared in church in a white lace wedding dress I had designed and made myself—a miniskirt!

How Asian Americans treat me with respect to my handicap tells me a great deal about their degree of acculturation. Recent immigrants behave just like Asians in Asia; those who have been here longer or who grew up in the United States behave more like their white counterparts. I have not encountered any distinctly Asian-American pattern of response. What makes the experience of Asian-American handicapped people unique is the quality of responses we elicit.

Regardless of racial or cultural background, most handicapped people have to learn to find a balance between the desire to attain physical independence and the need to take care of ourselves by not overtaxing our bodies. In my case, I've had to learn to accept the fact that leading an active life has its price. Between the ages of eight and eighteen, I walked without using crutches or braces, but the effort caused my right leg to become badly misaligned. Soon after I came to the United States, I had a series of operations to straighten out the bones of my right leg; afterwards though my leg looked straighter and presumably better, I could no longer walk on my own. Initially my doctors fitted me with a brace, but I found wearing one cumbersome and soon gave it up. I could move around much more easily—and more important, faster—by using one crutch. One orthopedist after another warned me that using a single crutch was a bad practice. They were right. Over the years my spine developed a double-S curve, and for the last twenty years I have suffered from severe, chronic back pains, which neither conventional physical therapy nor a lighter workload can eliminate.

The only thing that helps my backaches is a good massage, but the soothing effect lasts no more than a day or two. Massages are expensive, especially when one needs them three times a week. So I found a job that pays better, but at which I have to work longer hours, consequently increasing the physical strain on my body—a sort of vicious circle. When I was in my thirties, my doctors told me that if I kept leading the strenuous life I did, I would be in a wheelchair by the time I was forty. They were right on target: I bought myself a wheelchair when I was forty-one. But being the incorrigible character that I am, I use it only when I am *not* in a hurry!

It is a good thing, however, that I am too busy to think much about my handicap or my backaches because pain can physically debilitate as well as cause depression. And there are days when my spirits get rather low. What has helped me is realizing that being handicapped is akin to growing old at an accelerated rate. The contradiction I experience is that often my mind races along as though I'm only twenty while my body feels about sixty. But fifteen or twenty years hence, unlike my peers who will have to cope with aging for the first time, I shall be full of cheer because I will have already fought, and I hope won, that battle long ago. . . .

I've often wondered if I would have been a different person had I not been physically handicapped. I really don't know, though there is no question that being handicapped has marked me. But at the same time I usually do not *feel* handicapped—and consequently, I do not *act* handicapped. People are therefore less likely to treat me as a handicapped person. There is no doubt, however, that the lives of my parents, sister, husband, other family members, and some close friends have been affected by my physical condition. They have had to learn not to hide me away at home, not to feel embarrassed by how I look or react to people who say silly things to me, and not to resent me for the extra demands my condition makes on them. Perhaps the hardest thing for those who live with handicapped people is to know when and how to offer help. There are no guidelines applicable to all situations. My advice is, when in doubt, ask, but ask in a way that does not smack of pity or embarrassment. Most important, please don't talk to us as though we are children.

So, has being physically handicapped been a handicap? It all depends on one's attitude. Some years ago, I told a friend that I had once said to an affirmative action compliance officer (somewhat sardonically since I do not believe in the head-count approach to affirmative action) that the institution which employs me is triply lucky because it can count me as nonwhite, female and handicapped. He responded, "Why don't you tell them to count you four times? . . . Remember, you're short, besides!"

from The Case for Official English

S. I. Hayakawa

WHAT is it that has made a society out of the hodgepodge of nationalities, races, and colors represented in the immigrant hordes that people our nation? It is language, of course, that has made communication among all these elements possible. It is with a common language that we have dissolved distrust and fear. It is with language that we have drawn up the understandings and agreements and social contracts that make a society possible.

But while language is a necessary cause for our oneness as a society, it is not a sufficient cause. A foreigner cannot, by speaking faultless English, become an Englishman. Paul Theroux, a contemporary novelist and travel writer, has commented on this fact: "Foreigners are always aliens in England. No one becomes English. It's a very tribal society. . . . No one becomes Japanese. . . . No one becomes Nigerian. But Nigerians, Japanese, and English become Americans."

One need not speak faultless American English to become an American. Indeed, one may continue to speak English with an appalling foreign accent. This is true of some of my friends, but they are seen as fully American because of the warmth and enthusiasm with which they enter into the life of the communities in which they live. . . .

In the past several years, strong resistance to the "melting pot" idea has arisen, especially for those who claim to speak for the Hispanic peoples. Instead of a melting pot, they say, the national ideal should be a "salad bowl," in which different elements are thrown together but not "melted," so that the original ingredients retain their distinctive character. In addition to the increasing size of the Spanish-speaking population in our nation, two legislative actions have released this outburst of effort on behalf of the Spanish language and Hispanic culture.

First, there was the so-called "bilingual ballot" mandated in 1975 in an amendment to the Voting Rights Act, which required foreign language ballots when voters of selected language groups reached 5 percent or more in any voting district. The groups chosen to be so favored were Asian Americans (Chinese, Filipino, Japanese, Korean), American Indians, Alaskan Natives, and "peoples of Spanish heritage," that is, Puerto Ricans, Cubans, and Mexican Americans.

Sensitive as Americans have been to racism, especially since the days of the civil rights movement, no one seems to have noticed the profound racism expressed in the amendment that created the bilingual ballot. Brown people, like Mexicans and Puerto Ricans, red people, like American Indians, and yellow people, like the Japanese and Chinese, are assumed not to be smart enough to learn English. No provision is made, however, for non-English-speaking French-Canadians in Maine or Vermont, or for the Hebrew-speaking Hasidic Jews in Brooklyn, who are white and are presumed to be able to learn English without difficulty. Voters in San Francisco encountered ballots in Spanish and Chinese for the first time in the elections of 1980, much to their surprise, since authorizing legislation had been passed by Congress with almost no debate, no roll-call vote, and no public discussion. Naturalized Americans, who had taken the trouble to learn English to become citizens, were especially angry and remain so.

Furthermore, there was the *Lau* decision of the U.S. Supreme Court in response to a suit brought by a Chinese of San Francisco who complained that his children were not being taught English adequately in the public schools they were attending. Justice William O. Douglas, delivering the opinion of the court, wrote: "No specific remedy is urged upon us. Teaching English to the students of Chinese ancestry who do not speak the language is one choice. Giving instructions to this group in Chinese is another. There may be others. Petitioner asks only that the Board of Education be directed to apply its expertise to the problem and rectify the situation." Justice Douglas's decision, concurred in by the entire court, granted the *Lau* petition. Because the *Lau* decision did not specify the method by which English was to be taught, it turned out to be a go-ahead for amazing educational developments, not so much for the Chinese as for Hispanics, who appropriated the decision and took it to apply especially to themselves.

The new U.S. Department of Education, established during the Carter administration, was eager to make its presence known by expanding its bureaucracy and its influence. The department quickly announced a vast program with federal funding for bilingual education, which led to the hiring of Spanish-speaking teachers by the thousands. The department furthermore issued what were known as the Lau Regulations, which required under the threat of withdrawal of federal funds that (1) non-English-speaking pupils be taught English, and that (2) academic subjects be taught in the pupils' own language. The contradiction between these two regulations seems not to have occurred to the educational theorists in the Department of Education. Nor does it seem to trouble, to this day, the huge membership of the National Association for Bilingual Education.

Bilingual education rapidly became a growth industry, requiring more and more teachers. Complaints began to arise from citizens that "bilingual education" was not bilingual at all, since many Spanish-speaking teachers hired for the program were found not to be able to speak English. Despite the ministrations of the Department of Education, or perhaps because of them, Hispanic students to a shocking degree drop out of school, educated neither in Hispanic nor in American language and culture. "Hispanics are the least educated minority in America, according to a report by the American Council on Education," writes Earl Byrd. "The report says 50 percent of all Hispanic youths in America drop out of high school, and only 7 percent finish college. Twelve percent of black youths and 23 percent of whites finish college. Eighteen percent of all Hispanics in America who are 25 or older are classified as functional illiterates, compared to 10 percent for blacks and 3 percent for whites."

I welcome the Hispanic—and as a Californian, I welcome especially the Mexican—influence on our culture. My wife was wise enough to insist that both our son and daughter learn Spanish as children and to keep reading Spanish as they were growing up. Consequently, my son, a newspaperman, was able to work for six months as an exchange writer for a newspaper in Costa Rica, while a Costa Rican reporter took my son's place in Oregon. My daughter, a graduate of the University of California at Santa Cruz, speaks Spanish, French, and after a year in Monterey Language School, Japanese.

The ethnic chauvinism of the present Hispanic leadership is an unhealthy trend in present-day America. It threatens a division perhaps more ominous in the long run than the division between blacks and whites. Blacks and whites have problems enough with each other, to be sure, but they quarrel with each other in one language. Even Malcolm X, in his fiery denunciations of the racial situation in America, wrote excellent and eloquent English. But the present politically ambitious "Hispanic Caucus" looks forward to a destiny for Spanish-speaking Americans separate from that of Anglo-, Italian-, Polish-, Greek-, Lebanese-, Chinese-, and Afro-Americans, and all the rest of us who rejoice in our ethnic diversity, which gives us our richness as a culture, and the English language, which keeps us in communication with each other to create a unique and vibrant culture . . . .

from
When Heaven and Earth Changed Places

Le Ly Hayslip

AFTER my brother Bon went North, I began to pay more attention to my father.

He was built solidly—big boned—for a Vietnamese man, which meant he probably had well-fed, noble ancestors. People said he had the body of a natural-born warrior. He was a year younger and an inch shorter than my mother, but just as good-looking. His face was round, like a Khmer or Thai, and his complexion was brown as soy from working all his life in the sun. He was very easygoing about everything and seldom in a hurry. Seldom, too, did he say no to a request—from his children or his neighbors. Although he took everything in stride, he was a hard and diligent worker. Even on holidays, he was always mending things or tending to our house and animals. He would not wait to be asked for help if he saw someone in trouble. Similarly, he always said what he thought, although he knew, like most honest men, when to keep silent. Because of his honesty, his empathy, and his openness to people, he understood life deeply. Perhaps that is why he was so easygoing. Only a half-trained mechanic thinks everything needs fixing.

He loved to smoke cigars and grew a little tobacco in our yard. My mother always wanted him to sell it, but there was hardly ever enough to take to market. I think for her it was the principle of the thing: smoking cigars was like burning money. Naturally, she had a song for such gentle vices—her own habit of chewing betel nuts included:

> *Get rid of your tobacco,*
> *And you will get a water buffalo.*
> *Give away your betel,*
> *And you will get more paddy land.*

Despite her own good advice, she never abstained from chewing betel, nor my father from smoking cigars. They were rare luxuries that life and the war allowed them.

My father also liked rice wine, which we made, and enjoyed an occasional beer, which he purchased when there was nothing else we needed. After he'd had a few sips, he would tell jokes and happy stories, and the village kids would flock around. Because I was his youngest daughter, I was entitled to listen from his knee—the place of honor. Sometimes he would sing funny songs about whoever threatened the village, and we would feel better. For example, when the French or Moroccan soldiers were near, he would sing:

> *There are many kinds of vegetables;*
> *Why do you like spinach?*
> *There are many kinds of wealth;*
> *Why do you use Minh money?*
> *There are many kinds of people;*
> *Why do you love terrorists?*

We laughed because these were all the things the French told us about the Viet Minh fighters whom we favored in the war. Years later, when the Viet Cong were near, he would sing:

> *There are many kinds of vegetables;*
> *Why do you like spinach?*
> *There are many kinds of money;*
> *Why do you use Yankee dollars?*
> *There are many kinds of people;*
> *Why do you disobey your ancestors?*

This was funny because the words were taken from the speeches the North Vietnamese cadres delivered to shame us for helping the Republic. He used to have a song for when the Viet Minh were near too, which asked in the same way, "Why do you use francs?" and "Why do you love French traitors?" Because he sang these songs with a comical voice, my mother never appreciated them. She couldn't see the absurdity of our situation as clearly as we children. To her, war and real life were different. To us, they were all the same.

Even as a parent, my father was more lenient than our mother, and we sometimes ran to him for help when she was angry. Most of the time it didn't work, and he would lovingly rub our heads as we were dragged off to be spanked. The village saying went: "A naughty child learns more from a whipping stick than a sweet stick." We children were never quite sure about that but agreed the whipping stick was an eloquent teacher. When he absolutely had to punish us himself, he didn't waste time. Wordlessly, he would find a long, supple bamboo stick and let us have it behind our thighs. It stung, but he could have whipped us harder. I think seeing the pain in his face hurt more than receiving his halfhearted blows. Because of that, we seldom did anything to merit a father's spanking—the highest penalty in our family. Violence in any form offended him. For this reason, I think he grew old before his time.

One of the few times my father ever touched my mother in a way not consistent with love was during one of the yearly floods, when people came to our village for safety from the lower ground. We sheltered many in our house, which was nothing more than a two-room hut with woven mats for a floor. I came home one day in winter rain to see refugees and Republican soldiers milling around outside. They did not know I lived there, so I had to elbow my way inside. It was nearly suppertime, and I knew my mother would be fixing as much food as we could spare.

In the part of the house we used as our kitchen, I discovered my mother crying. She and my father had gotten into an argument outside a few minutes before. He had assured the refugees he would find something to eat for everyone, and she insisted there would not be enough for her children if everyone was fed. He repeated his order to her, this time loud enough for all to hear. Naturally, he thought this would end the argument. She persisted in contradicting him, so he had slapped her.

This show of male power—we called it do danh vo—was usual behavior for Vietnamese husbands but unusual for my father. My mother could be as strict as she wished with his children, and he would seldom interfere. Now, I discovered there were limits even to his great patience. I saw the glowing red mark on her cheek and asked if she was crying because it hurt. She said no. She said she was crying because her action had caused my father to lose face in front of strangers. She promised that if I ever did what she had done to a husband, I would have both cheeks glowing: one from his blow and one from hers.

Once, when I was the only child at home, my mother went to Danang to visit Uncle Nhu, and my father had to take care of

me. I woke up from my nap in the empty house and cried for my
mother. My father came in from the yard and reassured me, but
I was still cranky and continued crying. Finally, he gave me a
rice cookie to shut me up. Needless to say, this was a tactic my
mother never used.

The next afternoon I woke up, and although I was not feeling
cranky, I thought a rice cookie might be nice. I cried a fake cry,
and my father came running in.

"What's this?" he asked, making a worried face. "Little Bay Ly
doesn't want a cookie?"

I was confused again.

"Look under your pillow," he said with a smile.

I twisted around and saw that, while I was sleeping, he had
placed a rice cookie under my pillow. We both laughed, and he
picked me up like a sack of rice and carried me outside while I
gobbled the cookie.

In the yard, he plunked me down under a tree and told me
some stories. After that, he got some scraps of wood and showed
me how to make things: a doorstop for my mother and a toy duck
for me. This was unheard of—a father doing these things with a
child that was not a son! Where my mother would instruct me on
cooking and cleaning and tell stories about brides, my father
showed me the mystery of hammers and explained the customs
of our people.

His knowledge of the Vietnamese went back to the Chinese
Wars in ancient times. I learned how one of my distant ancestors, a woman named Phung Thi Chinh, led Vietnamese fighters
against the Han. In one battle, even though she was pregnant
and surrounded by Chinese, she delivered the baby, tied it to
her back, and cut her way to safety wielding a sword in each
hand. I was amazed at this warrior's bravery and impressed
that I was her descendant. Even more, I was amazed and impressed by my father's pride in her accomplishments (she was,
after all, a humble female), and his belief that I was worthy of
her example. *"Con phai theo got chan co ta"* (Follow in her footsteps), he said. Only later would I learn what he truly meant.

Never again did I cry after my nap. Phung Thi women were
too strong for that. Besides, I was my father's daughter, and we
had many things to do together.

On the eve of my mother's return, my father cooked a feast of
roast duck. When we sat down to eat it, I felt guilty, and my

feelings showed on my face. He asked why I acted so sad.

"You've killed one of mother's ducks," I said. "One of the fat kind she sells at the market. She says the money buys gold which she saves for her daughters' weddings. Without gold for a dowry—*con o gia*—I will be an old maid!"

My father looked suitably concerned, then brightened and said, "Well, Bay Ly, if you can't get married, you will just have to live at home forever with me!"

I clapped my hands at the happy prospect.

My father cut into the rich, juicy bird and said, "Even so, we won't tell your mother about the duck, okay?"

I giggled and swore myself to secrecy.

The next day, I took some water out to him in the fields. My mother was due home any time, and I used every opportunity to step outside and watch for her. My father stopped working, drank gratefully, then took my hand and led me to the top of a nearby hill. It had a good view of the village and the land beyond it, almost to the ocean. I thought he was going to show me my mother coming back, but he had something else in mind.

He said, "Bay Ly, you see all this here? This is the Vietnam we have been talking about. You understand that a country is more than a lot of dirt, rivers, and forests, don't you?"

I said, "Yes, I understand." After all, we had learned in school that one's country is as sacred as a father's grave.

"Good. You know, some of these lands are battlefields where your brothers and cousins are fighting. They may never come back. Even your sisters have all left home in search of a better life. You are the only one left in my house. If the enemy comes back, you must be both a daughter and a son. I told you how the Chinese used to rule our land. People in this village had to risk their lives diving in the ocean just to find pearls for the Chinese emperor's gown. They had to risk tigers and snakes in the jungle just to find herbs for his table. Their payment for this hardship was a bowl of rice and another day of life. That is why Le Loi, Gia Long, the Trung sisters, and Phung Thi Chinh fought so hard to expel the Chinese. When the French came, it was the same old story. Your mother and I were taken to Danang to build a runway for their airplanes. We labored from sunup to sundown and well after dark. If we stopped to rest or have a smoke, a Moroccan would come up and whip our behinds. Our reward was a bowl of rice and another day of life. Freedom is never a gift, Bay Ly. It must be won and won again. Do you understand?"

I said that I did.

"Good." He moved his finger from the patchwork of brown dikes, silver water, and rippling stalks to our house at the edge of the village. "This land here belongs to me. Do you know how I got it?"

I thought a moment, trying to remember my mother's stories, then said honestly, "I can't remember."

He squeezed me lovingly. "I got it from your mother."

"What? That can't be true!" I said. Everyone in the family knew my mother was poor and my father's family was wealthy. Her parents were dead, and she had to work like a slave for her mother-in-law to prove herself worthy. Such women don't have land to give away!

"It's true." My father's smile widened. "When I was a young man, my parents needed someone to look after their lands. They had to be very careful about who they chose as wives for their three sons. In the village, your mother had a reputation as the hardest worker of all. She raised herself and her brothers without parents. At the same time, I noticed a beautiful woman working in the fields. When my mother said she was going to talk to the matchmaker about this hard-working village girl she'd heard about, my heart sank. I was too attracted to this mysterious tall woman I had seen in the rice paddies. You can imagine my surprise when I found out the girl my mother heard about and the woman I admired were the same.

"Well, we were married, and my mother tested your mother severely. She not only had to cook and clean and know everything about children, but she had to be able to manage several farms and know when and how to take the extra produce to the market. Of course, she was testing her other daughters-in-law as well. When my parents died, they divided their several farms among their sons, but you know what? They gave your mother and me the biggest share because they knew we would take care of it best. That's why I say the land came from her, because it did."

I suddenly missed my mother very much and looked down the road to the south, hoping to see her. My father noticed my sad expression.

"Hey." He poked me in the ribs. "Are you getting hungry for lunch?"

"No. I want to learn how to take care of the farm. What happens if the soldiers come back? What did you and Mother do when the soldiers came?"

My father squatted on the dusty hilltop and wiped the sweat from his forehead. "The first thing I did was to tell myself that it was my duty to survive—to take care of my family and my farm. That is a tricky job in wartime. It's as hard as being a soldier. The Moroccans were very savage. One day the rumor passed that they were coming to destroy the village. You may remember the night I sent you and your brothers and sisters away with your mother to Danang."

"You didn't go with us!" My voice still held the horror of the night I thought I had lost my father.

"Right! I stayed near the village—right on this hill—to keep an eye on the enemy and on our house. If they really wanted to destroy the village, I would save some of our things so that we could start over. Sure enough, that was their plan.

"The real problem was to keep things safe and avoid being captured. Their patrols were everywhere. Sometimes I went so deep in the forest that I worried about getting lost, but all I had to do was follow the smoke from the burning huts and I could find my way back.

"Once, I was trapped between two patrols that had camped on both sides of a river. I had to wait in the water for two days before one of them moved on. When I got out, my skin was shriveled like an old melon. I was so cold I could hardly move. From the waist down, my body was black with leeches. But it was worth all the pain. When your mother came back, we still had some furniture and tools to cultivate the earth. Many people lost everything. Yes, we were very lucky."

My father put his arms around me. "My brother Huong—your uncle Huong—had three sons and four daughters. Of his four daughters, only one is still alive. Of his three sons, two went north to Hanoi, and one went south to Saigon. Huong's house is very empty. My other brother, your uncle Luc, had only two sons. One went north to Hanoi; the other was killed in the fields. His daughter is deaf and dumb. No wonder he has taken to drink, eh? Who does he have to sing in his house and tend his shrine when he is gone? My sister Lien had three daughters and four sons. Three of the four sons went to Hanoi, and the fourth went to Saigon to find his fortune. The girls all tend their in-laws and mourn slain husbands. Who will care for Lien when she is too feeble to care for herself? Finally, my baby sister Nhien lost her husband to French bombers. Of her two sons, one went to Hanoi, and the other joined the Republic, then defected, then was murdered in his house. Nobody knows which side killed him. It doesn't really matter."

My father drew me out to arm's length and looked me squarely in the eye. "Now, Bay Ly, do you understand what your job is?"

I squared my shoulders and put on a soldier's face. "My job is to avenge my family. To protect my farm by killing the enemy. I must become a woman warrior like Phung Thi Chinh!"

My father laughed and pulled me close. "No, little peach blossom. Your job is to stay alive—to keep an eye on things and keep the village safe. To find a husband and have babies and tell the story of what you've seen to your children and anyone else who'll listen. Most of all, it is to live in peace and tend the shrine of our ancestors. Do these things well, Bay Ly, and you will be worth more than any soldier who ever took up a sword."

Kubota

Garrett Hongo

ON December 8, 1941, the day after the Japanese attack on Pearl Harbor in Hawaii, my grandfather barricaded himself with his family—my grandmother, my teenage mother, her two sisters and two brothers—inside of his home in La'ie, a sugar plantation village on Oahu's North Shore. This was my maternal grandfather, a man most villagers called by his last name, Kubota. It could mean either "Wayside Field" or else "Broken Dreams," depending on which ideograms he used. Kubota ran La'ie's general store, and the previous night, after a long day of bad news on the radio, some locals had come by, pounded on the front door, and made threats. One was said to have brandished a machete. They were angry and shocked, as the whole nation was in the aftermath of the surprise attack. Kubota was one of the few Japanese Americans in the village and president of the local Japanese language school. He had become a target for their rage and suspicion. A wise man, he locked all his doors and windows and did not open his store the next day, but stayed closed and waited for news from some official.

He was a *kibei*, a Japanese American born in Hawaii (a U.S. territory then, so he was thus a citizen) but who was subsequently sent back by his father for formal education in Hiroshima, Japan, their home province. *Kibei* is written with two ideograms in Japanese: one is the word for "return" and the other is the word for "rice." Poetically, it means one who returns from America, known as the Land of Rice in Japanese (by contrast, Chinese immigrants called their new home Mountain of Gold).

Kubota was graduated from a Japanese high school and then came back to Hawaii as a teenager. He spoke English—and a Hawaiian creole version of it at that—with a Japanese accent. But he was well liked and good at numbers, scrupulous and hard working like so many immigrants and children of immigrants. Castle & Cook, a grower's company that ran the sugarcane business along the North Shore, hired him on first as a stock boy and then appointed him to run one of its company stores. He did well, had the trust of management and labor—not an easy accomplishment in any day—married, had children, and had begun to exert himself in community affairs and excel in his own recreations. He put together a Japanese community organization that backed a Japanese language school for children and sponsored teachers from Japan. Kubota boarded many of them, in succession, in his own home. This made dinners a silent affair for his talkative, Hawaiian-bred children as their stern *sensei,* or teacher, was nearly always at table and their own abilities in the Japanese language were as delinquent as their attendance. While Kubota and the *sensei* rattled on about things Japanese, speaking Japanese, his children hurried through their suppers and tried to run off early to listen to the radio shows.

After dinner, while the *sensei* graded exams seated in a wicker chair in the spare room and his wife and children gathered around the radio in the front parlor, Kubota sat on the screened porch outside, reading the local Japanese newspapers. He finished reading about the same time as he finished the tea he drank for his digestion—a habit he'd learned in Japan—and then he'd get out his fishing gear and spread it out on the plank floors. The wraps on his rods needed to be redone, gears in his reels needed oil, and, once through with those tasks, he'd painstakingly wind on hundreds of yards of new line. Fishing was his hobby and his passion. He spent weekends camping along the North Shore beaches with his children, setting up umbrella tents, packing a rice pot and hibachi along for meals. And he caught fish. *Ulu'a* mostly, the huge surf-feeding fish known on the mainland as the jack crevalle, but he'd go after almost anything in its season. In Kawela, a plantation-owned bay nearby, he fished for mullet Hawaiian-style with a throw net, stalking the bottom-hugging, gray-backed schools as they gathered at the stream mouths and in the freshwater springs. In an outrigger out beyond the reef, he'd try for *aku*—the skipjack tuna prized for steaks and, sliced raw and mixed with fresh seaweed and cut onions, for *sashimi* salad. In Kahaluu and Ka'awa and on an offshore rock locals called Goat Island, he loved to go torching, stringing lanterns on bamboo poles stuck in the sand to attract *kumu'u,* the red goatfish, as they schooled at night just inside the reef. But in Lai'e on Laniloa Point near Kahuku, the northernmost tip of Oahu, he cast twelve- and fourteen-foot surf rods for the huge, varicolored, and fast-running *ulu'a* as they ran for schools of squid and baitfish just beyond the biggest breakers and past the low sand flats wadable from the shore to nearly a half mile out. At sunset, against the western light, he looked as if he walked on water as he came back, fish and rods slung over his shoulders, stepping along the rock and coral path just inches under the surface of a running tide.

When it was torching season, in December or January, he'd drive out the afternoon before and stay with old friends, the Tanakas or Yoshikawas, shopkeepers like him who ran stores near the fishing grounds. They'd have been preparing for weeks, selecting and cutting their bamboo poles, cleaning the hurricane lanterns, tearing up burlap sacks for the cloths they'd soak with kerosene and tie onto sticks they'd poke into the soft sand of the shallows. Once lit, touched off with a Zippo lighter, these would be the torches they'd use as beacons to attract the schooling fish. In another time, they might have made up a dozen paper lanterns of the kind mostly used for decorating the summer folk dances outdoors on the grounds of the Buddhist church during O-Bon, the Festival for the Dead. But now, wealthy and modern and efficient killers of fish, Tanaka and Kubota used rag torches and Colemans and cast rods with tips made of Tonkin bamboo and butts of American-spun fiberglass. After just one good night, they might bring back a prize bounty of a dozen burlap bags filled with scores of bloody, rigid fish delicious to eat and even better to give away as gifts to friends, family, and special customers.

It was a Monday night, the day after Pearl Harbor, and there was a rattling knock at the front door. Two FBI agents presented themselves, showed identification, and took my grandfather in for questioning in Honolulu. He didn't return home for days. No one knew what had happened or what was wrong. But there was a roundup going on of all those in the Japanese-American community suspected of sympathizing with the enemy and worse. My grandfather was suspected of espionage, of communicating with offshore Japanese submarines launched from the attack fleet days before war began. Torpedo planes and escort fighters, decorated with the insignia of the Rising Sun, had taken an approach route from northwest of Oahu directly across Kahuku Point and on toward Pearl. They had strafed an auxiliary air station near the fishing grounds my grandfather loved and destroyed a small gun battery there, killing three men. Kubota was known to have sponsored and harbored Japanese nationals in his own home. He had a radio. He had wholesale access to firearms. Circumstances and an undertone of racial resentment had combined with wartime hysteria in the aftermath of the tragic naval battle to cast suspicion on the loyalties of my grandfather and all other Japanese Americans. The FBI reached out and pulled hundreds of them in for questioning in dragnets cast throughout the West Coast and Hawaii.

My grandfather was lucky; he'd somehow been let go after only a few days. Others were not as fortunate. Hundreds, from small communities in Washington, California, Oregon, and Hawaii, were rounded up and, after what appeared to be routine questioning, shipped off under Justice Department orders to holding centers in Leuppe on the Navaho reservation in Arizona, in Fort Missoula in Montana, and on Sand Island in Honolulu Harbor. There were other special camps on Maui in Ha'iku and on Hawaii—the Big Island—in my own home village of Volcano.

Many of these men—it was exclusively the Japanese-American men suspected of ties to Japan who were initially rounded up—did not see their families again for more than four years. Under a suspension of due process that was only after the fact ruled as warranted by military necessity, they were, if only temporarily, "disappeared" in Justice Department prison camps scattered in particularly desolate areas of the United States designated as militarily "safe." These were grim forerunners of the assembly centers and concentration camps for the 120,000 Japanese-American evacuees that were to come later.

I am Kubota's eldest grandchild, and I remember him as a lonely, habitually silent old man who lived with us in our home near Los Angeles for most of my childhood and adolescence. It was the fifties, and my parents had emigrated from Hawaii to the mainland in the hope of a better life away from the old sugar plantation. After some success, they had sent back for my grandparents and taken them in. And it was my grandparents who did the work of the household while my mother and father worked their salaried city jobs. My grandmother cooked and sewed, washed our clothes, and knitted in the front room under the light of a huge lamp with a bright three-way bulb. Kubota raised a flower garden, read up on soils and grasses in gardening books, and planted a zoysia lawn in front and a dichondra one in back. He planted a small patch near the rear block wall with green onions, eggplant, white Japanese radishes, and cucumber. While he hoed and spaded the loamless, clayey earth of Los Angeles, he sang particularly plangent songs in Japanese about plum blossoms and bamboo groves.

Once, in the mid-sixties, after a dinner during which, as always, he had been silent while he worked away at a meal of fish and rice spiced with dabs of Chinese mustard and catsup thinned with soy sauce, Kubota took his own dishes to the kitchen sink and washed them up. He took a clean jelly jar out of the cupboard—the glass was thick and its shape squatty like an old-fashioned. He reached around to the hutch below where he kept his bourbon. He made himself a drink and retired to the living room where I was expected to join him for "talk story," the Hawaiian idiom for chewing the fat.

I was a teenager and, though I was bored listening to stories I'd heard often enough before at holiday dinners, I was dutiful. I took my spot on the couch next to Kubota and heard him out. Usually, he'd tell me about his schooling in Japan where he learned judo along with mathematics and literature. He'd learned the *soroban* there—the abacus, which was the original pocket calculator of the Far East—and that, along with his strong, judo-trained back, got him his first job in Hawaii. This was the moral. "Study *ha-ahd*," he'd say with pidgin emphasis. "Learn read good. Learn speak da kine *good* English." The message is the familiar one taught to any children of immigrants: succeed through education. And imitation. But this time, Kubota reached down into his past and told me a different story. I was thirteen by then, and I suppose he thought me ready for it. He told me about Pearl Harbor, how the planes flew in wing after wing of formations over his old house in La'ie in Hawaii, and how, the next day, after Roosevelt had made his famous "Day of Infamy" speech about the treachery of the Japanese, the FBI agents had come to his door and taken him in, hauled him off to Honolulu for questioning, and held him without charge for several days. I thought he was lying. I thought he was making up a kind of horror story to shock me and give his moral that much more starch. But it was true. I asked around. I brought it up during history class in junior high school, and my teacher, after silencing me and stepping me off to the back of the room, told me that it was indeed so. I asked my mother and she said it was true. I asked my schoolmates, who laughed and ridiculed me for being so ignorant. We lived in a Japanese-American community, and the parents of most of my classmates were the *nisei* who had been interned as teenagers all through the war. But there was a strange silence around all of this. There was a hush, as if one were invoking the ill powers of the dead when one brought it up. No one cared to speak about the evacuation and relocation for very long. It wasn't in our history books, though we were studying World War II at the time. It wasn't in the family albums of the people I knew and whom I'd visit staying over weekends with friends. And it wasn't anything that the family talked about or allowed me to keep bringing up either. I was given the facts, told sternly and pointedly that "it was war" and that "nothing could be done." *"Shikatta ga nai"* is the phrase in Japanese, a kind of resolute and determinist pronouncement on how to deal with inexplicable tragedy. I was to know it but not to dwell on it. Japanese Americans were busy trying to forget it ever happened and were having a hard enough time building their new lives after "camp." It was as if we had no history for four years and the relocation was something unspeakable.

But Kubota would not let it go. In session after session, for months it seemed, he pounded away at his story. He wanted to tell me the names of the FBI agents. He went over their questions and his responses again and again. He'd tell me how one would try to act friendly toward him, offering his cigarettes while the other, who hounded him with accusations and threats, left the interrogation room. Good cop, bad cop, I thought to myself, already superficially streetwise from stories black classmates told of the Watts riots and from my having watched too many episodes of *Dragnet* and *The Mod Squad.* But Kubota was not interested in my experiences. I was not made yet, and he was determined that his stories be part of my making. He spoke quietly at first, mildly, but once into his narrative and after his drink was down, his voice would rise and quaver with resentment and he'd make his accusations. He gave his testimony to me and I held it at first cautiously in my conscience like it was an heirloom too delicate to expose to strangers and anyone outside of the world Kubota made with his words. "I give you story now," he once said, "and you learn speak good, eh?" It was my job, as the disciple of his preaching I had then become, Ananda to his Buddha, to reassure him with a promise. "You learn speak good like the Dillingham," he'd say another time, referring to the wealthy scion of the grower family who had once run, unsuccessfully, for one of Hawaii's first senatorial seats. Or he'd then invoke a magical name, the name of one of his heroes, a man he thought particularly exemplary and righteous. "Learn speak dah good Ing-rish like *Mistah Inouye*," Kubota shouted. "He *lick* dah Dillingham even in debate. I saw on *terre-bision* myself." He was remembering the debates before the first senatorial election just before

Hawaii was admitted to the Union as its fiftieth state. "You *tell* story," Kubota would end. And I had my injunction.

The town we settled in after the move from Hawaii is called Gardena, the independently incorporated city south of Los Angeles and north of San Pedro harbor. At its northern limit, it borders on Watts and Compton, black towns. To the southwest are Torrance and Redondo Beach, white towns. To the rest of L.A., Gardena is primarily famous for having legalized five-card draw poker after the war. On Vermont Boulevard, its eastern border, there is a dingy little Vegas-like strip of card clubs with huge parking lots and flickering neon signs that spell out "The Rainbow" and "The Horseshoe" in timed sequences of varicolored lights. The town is only secondarily famous as the largest community of Japanese Americans in the United States outside of Honolulu, Hawaii. When I was in high school there, it seemed to me that every *sansei* kid I knew wanted to be a doctor, an engineer, or a pharmacist. Our fathers were gardeners or electricians or nurserymen or ran small businesses catering to other Japanese Americans. Our mothers worked in civil service for the city or as cashiers for Thrifty Drug. What the kids wanted was a good job, good pay, a fine home, and no troubles. No one wanted to mess with the law—from either side—and no one wanted to mess with language or art. They all talked about getting into the right clubs so that they could go to the right schools. There was a certain kind of sameness, an intensely enforced system of conformity. Style was all. Boys wore moccasin-sewn shoes from Flagg Brothers, black A-1 slacks, and Kensington shirts with high collars. Girls wore their hair up in stiff bouffants solidified in hairspray and knew all the latest dances from the slauson to the funky chicken. We did well in chemistry and in math, no one who was Japanese but me spoke in English class or in history unless called upon, and no one talked about World War II. The day after Robert Kennedy was assassinated, after winning the California Democratic primary, we worked on calculus and elected class coordinators for the prom, featuring the 5th Dimension. We avoided grief. We avoided government. We avoided strong feelings and dangers of any kind. Once punished, we tried to maintain a concerted emotional and social discipline and would not willingly seek to fall out of the narrow margin of protective favor again.

But when I was thirteen, in junior high, I'd not understood why it was so difficult for my classmates, those who were themselves Japanese American, to talk about relocation. They had cringed, too, when I tried to bring it up during our discussions of World War II. I was Hawaiian-born. They were mainland-born. Their parents had been in camp, had been the ones to suffer the complicated experience of having to distance themselves from their own history and all things Japanese in order to make their way back and into the American social and economic mainstream. It was out of this sense of shame and a fear of stigma I was only beginning to understand that the *nisei* had silenced themselves. And, for their children, among whom I grew up, they wanted no heritage, no culture, no contact with a defiled history. I recall the silence very well. The Japanese-American children around me were burdened in a way I was not. Their injunction was silence. Mine was to speak.

Away at college, in another protected world in its own way as magical to me as the Hawaii of my childhood, I dreamed about my grandfather. Tired from studying languages, practicing German conjugations or scripting an army's worth of Chinese ideograms on a single sheet of paper, Kubota would come to me as I drifted off into sleep. Or I would walk across the newly mown ball field in back of my dormitory, cutting through a street-side phalanx of ancient eucalyptus trees on my way to visit friends off campus, and I would think of him, his anger, and his sadness.

I don't know myself what makes someone feel that kind of need to have a story they've lived through be deposited somewhere, but I can guess. I think about *The Illiad, The Odyssey, The Peloponnesian Wars* of Thucydides, and a myriad of the works of literature I've studied. A character, almost a *topoi* he occurs so often, is frequently the witness who gives personal testimony about an event the rest of his community cannot even imagine. The sibyl is such a character. And Procne, the maid whose tongue is cut out so that she will not tell that she has been raped by her own brother-in-law, the king of Thebes. There are the dime novels, the epic blockbusters Hollywood makes into miniseries, and then there are the plain, relentless stories of witnesses who have suffered through horrors major and minor that have marked and changed their lives. I myself haven't talked to Holocaust victims. But I've read their survival stories and their stories of witness and been revolted and moved by them. My father-in-law, Al Thiessen, tells me his war stories again and again and I listen. A Menonite who set aside the strictures of his own church in order to serve, he was a Marine codeman in the Pacific during World War II, in the Signal Corps on Guadalcanal,

Morotai, and Bougainville. He was part of the island-hopping maneuver MacArthur had devised to win the war in the Pacific. He saw friends die from bombs which exploded not ten yards away. When he was with the 298th Signal Corps attached to the Thirteenth Air Force, he saw plane after plane come in and crash, just short of the runway, killing their crews, setting the jungle ablaze with oil and gas fires. Emergency wagons would scramble, bouncing over newly bulldozed land men used just the afternoon before for a football game. Every time we go fishing together, whether it's in a McKenzie boat drifting for salmon in Tillamook Bay or taking a lunch break from wading the riffles of a stream in the Cascades, he tells me about what happened to him and the young men in his unit. One was a Jewish boy from Brooklyn. One was a foul-mouthed kid from Kansas. They died. And he *has* to tell me. And I *have* to listen. It's a ritual payment the young owe their elders who have survived. The evacuation and relocation is something like that.

Kubota, my grandfather, had been ill with Alzheimer's disease for some time before he died. At the house he'd built on Kame-hameha Highway in Hau'ula, a seacoast village just down the road from La'ie where he had his store, he'd wander out from the garage or greenhouse where he'd set up a workbench, and trudge down to the beach or up toward the line of pines he'd planted while employed by the Work Projects Administration during the thirties. Kubota thought he was going fishing. Or he thought he was back at work for Roosevelt, planting pines as a windbreak or soilbreak on the windward flank of the Ko'olau Mountains, emerald monoliths rising out of sea and cane fields from Waialua to Kaneohe. When I visited, my grandmother would send me down to the beach to fetch him. Or I'd run down Kam Highway a quarter mile or so and find him hiding in the cane field by the roadside, counting stalks, measuring circum-ferences in the claw of his thumb and forefinger. The look on his face was confused or concentrated, I didn't know which. But I guessed he was going fishing again. I'd grab him and walk him back to his house on the highway. My grandmother would shut him in a room.

Within a few years, Kubota had a stroke and survived it, then he had another one and was completely debilitated. The family decided to put him in a nursing home in Kahuku, just set back from the highway, within a mile or so of Kahuku Point and the Tanaka Store where he had his first job as a stock boy. He lived there three years, and I visited him once with my aunt. He was like a potato that had been worn down by cooking. Everything on him—his eyes, his teeth, his legs and torso—seemed like it had been sloughed away. What he had been was mostly gone now and I was looking at the nub of a man. In a wheelchair, he grasped my hands and tugged on them—violently. His hands were still thick and, I believed, strong enough to lift me out of my own seat into his lap. He murmured something in Japanese— he'd long ago ceased to speak any English. My aunt and I cried a little, and we left him.

I remember walking out on the black asphalt of the parking lot of the nursing home. It was heat-cracked and eroded already, and grass had veined itself into the interstices. There were coconut trees around, a cane field I could see across the street, and the ocean I knew was pitching a surf just beyond it. The green Ko'olaus came up behind us. Somewhere nearby, alongside the beach, there was an abandoned airfield in the middle of the canes. As a child, I'd come upon it playing one day, and my friends and I kept returning to it, day after day, playing war or sprinting games or coming to fly kites. I recognize it even now when I see it on TV—it's used as a site for action scenes in the detective shows Hollywood always sets in the islands: a helicopter chasing the hero racing away in a Ferrari, or gun dealers making a clandestine rendezvous on the abandoned runway. It was the old airfield strafed by Japanese planes the day the major flight attacked Pearl Harbor. It was the airfield the FBI thought my grandfather had targeted in his night fishing and signaling with the long surf poles he'd stuck in the sandy bays near Kahuku Point.

Kubota died a short while after I visited him, but not, I thought, without giving me a final message. I was on the mainland, in California studying for Ph.D. exams, when my grandmother called me with the news. It was a relief. He'd suffered from his debilitation a long time and I was grateful he'd gone. I went home for the funeral and gave the eulogy. My grandmother and I took his ashes home in a small, heavy metal box wrapped in a black *furoshiki*, a large silk scarf. She showed me the name the priest had given to him on his death, scripted with a calligraphy brush on a long, narrow talent of plain wood. Buddhist commoners, at death, are given priestly names, received symbolically into the clergy. The idea is that, in their next life, one of scholarship and leisure, they might meditate and attain the enlightenment the religion is aimed at. *"Shaku Shūchi,"* the ideograms read. It was Kubota's Buddhist name, incorporating characters from his family and given names. It meant "Shining Wisdom of the Law." He died on Pearl Harbor Day, December 7, 1983.

After years, after I'd finally come back to live in Hawaii again, only once did I dream of Kubota, my grandfather. It was the same night I'd heard HR 442, the redress bill for Japanese Americans, had been signed into law. In my dream that night Kubota was "torching," and he sang a Japanese song, a querulous and wavery folk ballad, as he hung paper lanterns on bamboo poles stuck into the sand in the shallow water of the lagoon behind the reef near Kahuku Point. Then he was at a work table, smoking a hand-rolled cigarette, letting it dangle from his lips Bogart-style as he drew, daintily and skillfully, with a narrow trim brush, ideogram after ideogram on a score of paper lanterns he had hung in a dark shed to dry. He had painted a talismanic mantra onto each lantern, the ideogram for the word "red" in Japanese, a bit of art blended with some superstition, a piece of sympathetic magic appealing to the magenta coloring on the rough skins of the schooling, night-feeding fish he wanted to attract to his baited hooks. He strung them from pole to pole in the dream then, hiking up his khaki worker's pants so his white ankles showed and wading through the shimmering black waters of the sand flats and then the reef. "The moon is leaving, leaving," he sang in Japanese. "Take me deeper in the savage sea." He turned and crouched like an ice racer then, leaning forward so that his unshaven face almost touched the light film of water. I could see the light stubble of beard like a fine, gray ash covering the lower half of his face. I could see his gold-rimmed spectacles. He held a small wooden boat in his cupped hands and placed it lightly on the sea and pushed it away. One of his lanterns was on it and, written in small neat rows like a sutra scroll, it had been decorated with the silvery names of all our dead.

from
Farewell to Manzanar

Jeanne Wakatsuki Houston and James Houston

IN December of 1941 Papa's disappearance didn't bother me nearly so much as the world I soon found myself in.

He had been a jack-of-all-trades. When I was born, he was farming near Inglewood. Later, when he started fishing, we moved to Ocean Park, near Santa Monica, and until they picked him up, that's where we lived, in a big frame house with a brick fireplace, a block back from the beach. We were the only Japanese family in the neighborhood. Papa liked it that way. He didn't want to be labeled or grouped by anyone. But with him gone and no way of knowing what to expect, my mother moved all of us down to Terminal Island. Woody already lived there, and one of my older sisters had married a Terminal Island boy. Mama's first concern now was to keep the family together; and once the war began, she felt safer there than isolated racially in Ocean Park. But for me, at age seven, the island was a country as foreign as India or Arabia would have been. It was the first time I had lived among other Japanese, or gone to school with them, and I was terrified all the time.

This was partly Papa's fault. One of his threats to keep us younger kids in line was "I'm going to sell you to the Chinaman." When I had entered kindergarten two years earlier, I was the only Oriental in the class. They sat me next to a Caucasian girl who happened to have very slanted eyes. I looked at her and began to scream, certain Papa had sold me out at last. My fear of her ran so deep I could not speak of it, even to Mama, couldn't explain why I was screaming. For two weeks I had nightmares about this girl, until the teachers finally moved me to the other side of the room. And it was still with me, this fear of Oriental faces, when we moved to Terminal Island.

In those days it was a company town, a ghetto owned and controlled by the canneries. The men went after fish, and whenever the boats came back—day or night—the women would be called to process the catch while it was fresh. One in the afternoon or four in the morning, it made no difference. My mother had to go to work right after we moved there. I can still hear the whistle—two toots for French's, three for Van Camp's—and she and Chizu would be out of bed in the middle of the night, heading for the cannery.

The house we lived in was nothing more than a shack, a barracks with single plank walls and rough wooden floors, like the cheapest kind of migrant workers' housing. The people around us were hard-working, boisterous, a little proud of their nickname, *yo-go-re,* which meant literally uncouth one, or roughneck, or dead-end kid. They not only spoke Japanese exclusively, they spoke a dialect peculiar to Kyushu, where their families had come from in Japan, a rough, fisherman's language, full of oaths and insults. Instead of saying *ba-ka-ta-re,* a common insult meaning stupid, Terminal Islanders would say *ba-ka-ya-ro,* a coarser and exclusively masculine use of the word, which implies gross stupidity. They would swagger and pick on outsiders and persecute anyone who didn't speak as they did. That was what made my own time there so hateful. I had never spoken anything but English, and the other kids in the second grade despised me for it. They were tough and mean, like ghetto kids anywhere. Each day after school I dreaded their ambush. My brother Kiyo, three years older, would wait for me at the door, where we would decide whether to run straight home together, or split up, or try a new and unexpected route.

None of these kids ever actually attacked. It was the threat that frightened us, their fearful looks, and the noises they would make, like miniature samurai, in a language we couldn't understand.

At the time it seemed we had been living under the reign of fear for years. In fact, we lived there about two months. Late in February the navy decided to clear Terminal Island completely. Even though most of us were American-born, it was dangerous having that many Orientals so close to the Long Beach Naval Station, on the opposite end of the island. We had known something like this was coming. But, like Papa's arrest, not much could be done ahead of time. There were four of us kids still young enough to be living with Mama, plus Granny, her mother, sixty-five then, speaking no English, and nearly blind. Mama didn't know where else she could get work, and we had nowhere else to move *to.* On February 25 the choice was made for us. We were given forty-eight hours to clear out.

The secondhand dealers had been prowling around for weeks,

like wolves, offering humiliating prices for goods and furniture they knew many of us would have to sell sooner or later. Mama had left all but her most valuable possessions in Ocean Park, simply because she had nowhere to put them. She had brought along her pottery, her silver, heirlooms like the kimonos Granny had brought from Japan, tea sets, lacquered tables, and one fine old set of china, blue and white porcelain, almost translucent. On the day we were leaving, Woody's car was so crammed with boxes and luggage and kids we had just run out of room. Mama had to sell this china.

One of the dealers offered her fifteen dollars for it. She said it was a full setting for twelve and worth at least two hundred. He said fifteen was his top price. Mama started to quiver. Her eyes blazed up at him. She had been packing all night and trying to calm down Granny, who didn't understand why we were moving again and what all the rush was about. Mama's nerves were shot, and now navy jeeps were patrolling the streets. She didn't say another word. She just glared at this man, all the rage and frustration channeled at him through her eyes.

He watched her for a moment and said he was sure he couldn't pay more than seventeen fifty for that china. She reached into the red velvet case, took out a dinner plate, and hurled it at the floor right in front of his feet.

The man leaped back shouting, "Hey! Hey, don't do that! Those are valuable dishes!"

Mama took out another dinner plate and hurled it at the floor, then another and another, never moving, never opening her mouth, just quivering and glaring at the retreating dealer, with tears streaming down her cheeks. He finally turned and scuttled out the door, heading for the next house. When he was gone, she stood there smashing cups and bowls and platters until the whole set lay in scattered blue and white fragments across the wooden floor.

The American Friends Service helped us find a small house in Boyle Heights, another minority ghetto, in downtown Los Angeles, now inhabited briefly by a few hundred Terminal Island refugees. Executive Order 9066 had been signed by President Roosevelt, giving the War Department authority to define military areas in the western states and to exclude from them anyone who might threaten the war effort. There was a lot of talk about internment, or moving inland, or something like that in store for all Japanese Americans. I remember my brothers sitting around the table talking very intently about what we were going to do, how we would keep the family together. They had seen how quickly Papa was removed, and they knew now that he would not be back for quite a while. Just before leaving Terminal Island Mama had received her first letter, from Bismarck, North Dakota. He had been imprisoned at Fort Lincoln, in an all-male camp for enemy aliens.

Papa had been the patriarch. He had always decided everything in the family. With him gone, my brothers, like councilors in the absence of a chief, worried about what should be done. The ironic thing is, there wasn't much left to decide. These were mainly days of quiet, desperate waiting for what seemed at the time to be inevitable. There is a phrase the Japanese use in such situations, when something difficult must be endured. You would hear the older heads, the issei, telling others very quietly, *"Shikata ga nai"* (It cannot be helped). *"Shikata ga nai"* (It must be done).

Mama and Woody went to work packing celery for a Japanese produce dealer. Kiyo and my sister May and I enrolled in the local school, and what sticks in my memory from those few weeks is the teacher—not her looks, her remoteness. In Ocean Park my teacher had been a kind, grandmotherly woman who used to sail with us in Papa's boat from time to time and who wept the day we had to leave. In Boyle Heights the teacher felt cold and distant. I was confused by all the moving and was having trouble with the classwork, but she would never help me out. She would have nothing to do with me.

This was the first time I had felt outright hostility from a Caucasian. Looking back, it is easy enough to explain. Public attitudes toward the Japanese in California were shifting rapidly. In the first few months of the Pacific war, America was on the run. Tolerance had turned to distrust and irrational fear. The hundred-year-old tradition of anti-Orientalism on the West Coast soon resurfaced, more vicious than ever. Its result became clear about a month later, when we were told to make our third and final move.

The name Manzanar meant nothing to us when we left Boyle Heights. We didn't know where it was or what it was. We went because the government ordered us to. And, in the case of my older brothers and sisters, we went with a certain amount of relief. They had all heard stories of Japanese homes being attacked, of beatings in the streets of California towns. They were as frightened of the Caucasians as Caucasians were of us. Moving, under what appeared to be government protection, to an area less directly threatened by the war seemed not such a bad idea at all. For some it actually sounded like a fine adventure.

Our pickup point was a Buddhist church in Los Angeles. It was very early, and misty, when we got there with our luggage. Mama had bought heavy coats for all of us. She grew up in eastern Washington and knew that anywhere inland in early April would be cold. I was proud of my new coat, and I remember sitting on a duffel bag trying to be friendly with the Greyhound driver. I smiled at him. He didn't smile back. He was befriending no one. Someone tied a numbered tag to my collar and to the duffel bag (each family was given a number, and that became our official designation until the camps were closed), someone else passed out box lunches for the trip, and we climbed aboard.

I had never been outside Los Angeles County, never traveled more than ten miles from the coast, had never even ridden on a bus. I was full of excitement, the way any kid would be, and wanted to look out the window. But for the first few hours the shades were drawn. Around me other people played cards, read magazines, dozed, waiting. I settled back, waiting too, and finally fell asleep. The bus felt very secure to me. Almost half its passengers were immediate relatives. Mama and my older brothers had succeeded in keeping most of us together, on the same bus, headed for the same camp. I didn't realize until much later what a job that was. The strategy had been, first, to have everyone living in the same district when the evacuation began, and then to get all of us included under the same family number, even though names had been changed by marriage. Many families weren't as lucky as ours and suffered months of anguish while trying to arrange transfers from one camp to another.

We rode all day. By the time we reached our destination, the shades were up. It was late afternoon. The first thing I saw was a yellow swirl across a blurred, reddish setting sun. The bus was being pelted by what sounded like splattering rain. It wasn't rain. This was my first look at something I would soon know very well, a billowing flurry of dust and sand churned up by the wind through Owens Valley.

We drove past a barbed-wire fence, through a gate, and into an open space where trunks and sacks and packages had been dumped from the baggage trucks that drove out ahead of us. I could see a few tents set up, the first rows of black barracks, and beyond them, blurred by sand, rows of barracks that seemed to spread for miles across this plain. People were sitting on cartons or milling around, with their backs to the wind, waiting to see which friends or relatives might be on this bus. As we approached, they turned or stood up, and some moved toward us expectantly. But inside the bus no one stirred. No one waved or spoke. They just stared out the windows, ominously silent. I didn't understand this. Hadn't we finally arrived, our whole family intact? I opened a window, leaned out, and yelled happily. "Hey! This whole bus is full of Wakatsukis!"

Outside, the greeters smiled. Inside there was an explosion of laughter, hysterical, tension-breaking laughter that left my brothers choking and whacking each other across the shoulders.

from

Sound-Shadows
of the New World

Ved Mehta

AT the airport, I was questioned by an immigration official.
"You're blind—totally blind—and they gave you a visa? You say
it's for your studies, but studies where?"

"At the Arkansas School for the Blind. It is in Little Rock, in
Arkansas."

He shuffled through the pages of a book. Sleep was in my eyes.
Drops of sweat were running down my back. My shirt and
trousers felt dirty.

"Arkansas School is not on our list of approved schools for
foreign students."

"I know," I said. "That is why the immigration officials in Delhi
gave me only a visitor's visa. They said that when I got to the
school I should tell the authorities to apply to be on your list of
approved schools, so that I could get a student visa." I showed
him a big manila envelope I was carrying; it contained my chest
x-rays, medical reports, and fingerprint charts, which were necessary for a student visa, and which I'd had prepared in advance.

"Why didn't you apply to an approved school in the first place
and come here on a proper student visa?" he asked, looking
through the material.

My knowledge of English was limited. With difficulty, I explained to him that I had applied to some thirty schools but
that, because I had been able to get little formal education in
India, the Arkansas School was the only one that would accept
me; that I had needed a letter of acceptance from an American
school to get dollars sanctioned by the Reserve Bank of India;
and that now that I was in America I was sure I could change
schools if the Arkansas School was not suitable or did not get
necessary approval.

Muttering to himself, the immigration official looked up at
me, down at his book, and up at me again. He finally announced, "I think you'll have to go to Washington and apply to

get your visa changed to a student visa before you can go to any school."

I recalled things that Daddyji used to say as we were growing up: "In life, there is only fight or flight. You must always fight," and "America is God's own country. People there are the most hospitable and generous people in the world." I told myself I had nothing to worry about. Then I remembered that Daddyji had mentioned a Mr. and Mrs. Dickens in Washington—they were friends of friends of his—and told me that I could get in touch with them in case of emergency.

"I will do whatever is necessary," I now said to the immigration official. "I will go to Washington."

He hesitated, as if he were thinking something, and then stamped my passport and returned it to me. "We Mehtas carry our luck with us," Daddyji used to say. He is right, I thought.

The immigration official suddenly became helpful, as if he were a friend. "You shouldn't have any trouble with the immigration people in Washington," he said, and asked, "Is anybody meeting you here?"

"Mr. and Mrs. di Francesco," I said.

Mrs. di Francesco was a niece of Manmath Nath Chatterjee, whom Daddyji had known when he himself was a student, in London, in 1920. Daddyji had asked Mr. Chatterjee, who had a Scottish-American wife and was now settled in Yellow Springs, Ohio, if he could suggest anyone with whom I might stay in New York, so that I could get acclimatized to America before proceeding to the Arkansas School, which was not due to open until the eleventh of September. Mr. Chatterjee had written back that, as it happened, his wife's niece was married to John di Francesco, a singer who was totally blind, and that Mr. and Mrs. di Francesco lived in New York, and would be delighted to meet me at the airport and keep me as a paying guest at fifteen dollars a week.

"How greedy of them to ask for money!" I had cried when I learned of the arrangement. "People come and stay with us for months and we never ask for an anna."

Daddyji had said, "In the West, people do not, as a rule, stay with relatives and friends but put up in hotels, or in houses as paying guests. That is the custom there. Mr. and Mrs. di Francesco are probably a young, struggling couple who could do with a little extra money."

The immigration official now came from behind the counter, led me to an open area, and shouted, with increasing volume,

"Francisco! . . . Franchesca! . . . De Franco!" I wasn't sure what the correct pronunciation was, but his shouting sounded really disrespectful. I asked him to call for Mr. and Mrs. di Francesco softly. He bellowed, "Di Fransesco!"

No one came. My mouth went dry. Mr. and Mrs. di Francesco had sent me such a warm invitation. I couldn't imagine why they would have let me down or what I should do next.

Then I heard the footsteps of someone running toward us. "Here I am. You must be Ved. I'm Muriel di Francesco. I'm sorry John couldn't come." I noted that the name was pronounced the way it was spelled, and that hers was a Yankee voice—the kind I had heard when I first encountered Americans at home, during the war—but it had the sweetness of the voices of my sisters.

We shook hands; she had a nice firm grip. I had an impulse to call her Auntie Muriel—at home, an older person was always called by an honorific, like "Auntie" or "Uncle"—but I greeted her as Daddyji had told me that Westerners liked to be greeted: "Mrs. di Francesco, I'm delighted to make your acquaintance."

Pearl Harbor Echoes in Seattle

Monica Sone

ON a peaceful Sunday morning, December 7, 1941, Henry, Sumi, and I were at choir rehearsal singing ourselves hoarse in preparation for the annual Christmas recital of Handel's "Messiah." Suddenly Chuck Mizuno, a young University of Washington student, burst into the chapel, gasping as if he had sprinted all the way up the stairs.

"Listen, everybody!" he shouted. "Japan just bombed Pearl Harbor . . . in Hawaii! It's war!"

The terrible words hit like a blockbuster, paralyzing us. Then we smiled feebly at each other, hoping this was one of Chuck's practical jokes. Miss Hara, our music director, rapped her baton impatiently on the music stand and chided him, "Now Chuck, fun's fun, but we have work to do. Please take your place. You're already half an hour late."

But Chuck strode vehemently back to the door, "I mean it, folks, honest! I just heard the news over my car radio. Reporters are talking a blue streak. Come on down and hear it for yourselves."

With that, Chuck swept out of the room, a swirl of young men following in his wake. Henry was one of them. The rest of us stayed, rooted to our places like a row of marionettes. I felt as if a fist had smashed my pleasant little existence, breaking it into jigsaw puzzle pieces. An old wound opened up again, and I found myself shrinking inwardly from my Japanese blood, the blood of an enemy. I knew instinctively that the fact that I was an American by birthright was not going to help me escape the consequences of this unhappy war.

One girl mumbled over and over again, "It can't be, God, it can't be!" Someone else was saying, "What a spot to be in! Do you think we'll be considered Japanese or Americans?"

A boy replied quietly, "We'll be Japs, same as always. But our parents are enemy aliens now, you know."

A shocked silence followed. Henry came for Sumi and me. "Come on, let's go home," he said.

We ran trembling to our car. Usually Henry was a careful driver, but that morning he bore down savagely on the accelerator. Boiling angry, he shot us up Twelfth Avenue, rammed through the busy Jackson Street intersection, and rocketed up the Beacon Hill bridge. We swung violently around to the left of the Marine Hospital and swooped to the top of the hill. Then Henry slammed on the brakes and we rushed helter-skelter up to the house to get to the radio. Asthma skidded away from under our trampling feet.

Mother was sitting limp in the huge armchair as if she had collapsed there, listening dazedly to the turbulent radio. Her face was frozen still, and the only words she could utter were, *"Komatta neh, komatta neh.* How dreadful, how dreadful."

Henry put his arms around her. She told him she first heard about the attack on Pearl Harbor when one of her friends phoned her and told her to turn on the radio.

We pressed close against the radio, listening stiffly to the staccato outbursts of an excited reporter: "The early morning sky of Honolulu was filled with the furious buzzing of Jap Zero planes for nearly three hours, raining death and destruction on the airfields below. . . . A warship anchored beyond the Harbor was sunk. . . ."

We were switched to the White House. The fierce clack of teletype machines and the babble of voices surging in and out from the background almost drowned out the speaker's terse announcements.

With every fiber of my being I resented this war. I felt as if I were on fire. "Mama, they should never have done it," I cried. "Why did they do it? Why? Why?"

Mother's face turned paper white. "What do you know about it? Right or wrong, the Japanese have been chafing with resentment for years. It was bound to happen, one time or another. You're young, Ka-chan, you know very little about the ways of nations. It's not as simple as you think, but this is hardly the time to be quarreling about it, is it?"

"No, it's too late, too late!" and I let the tears pour down my face.

Father rushed home from the hotel. He was deceptively calm as he joined us in the living room. Father was a born skeptic, and he believed nothing unless he could see, feel and smell it. He regarded all newspapers and radio news with deep suspicion. He shook his head doubtfully, "It must be propaganda. With the way things are going now between America and Japan, we should expect the most fantastic rumors, and this is one of the wildest I've heard yet." But we noticed that he was firmly glued to the radio. It seemed as if the regular Sunday programs, sounding off relentlessly hour after hour on schedule, were trying to blunt the catastrophe of the morning.

The telephone pealed nervously all day as people searched for comfort from each other. Chris called, and I told her how miserable and confused I felt about the war. Understanding as always, Chris said, "You know how I feel about you and your family, Kaz. Don't, for heaven's sake, feel the war is going to make any difference in our relationship. It's not your fault, nor mine! I wish to God it could have been prevented." Minnie called off her Sunday date with Henry. Her family was upset and they thought she should stay close to home instead of wandering downtown.

Late that night Father got a shortwave broadcast from Japan. Static sputtered, then we caught a faint voice, speaking rapidly in Japanese. Father sat unmoving as a rock, his head cocked. The man was talking about the war between Japan and America. Father bit his lips and Mother whispered to him anxiously, "It's true then, isn't it, Papa? It's true?"

Father was muttering to himself, "So they really did it!" Now having heard the news in their native tongue, the war had become a reality to Father and Mother.

"I suppose from now on, we'll hear about nothing but the humiliating defeats of Japan in the papers here," Mother said, resignedly.

Henry and I glared indignantly at Mother, then Henry shrugged his shoulders and decided to say nothing. Discussion of politics, especially Japan versus America, had become taboo in our family for it sent tempers skyrocketing. Henry and I used to criticize Japan's aggressions in China and Manchuria while Father and Mother condemned Great Britain and America's superior attitude toward Asiatics and their interference with Japan's economic growth. During these arguments, we had eyed each other like strangers, parents against children. They left us with a hollow feeling at the pit of the stomach.

Just then the shrill peel of the telephone cut off the possibility of a family argument. When I answered, a young girl's voice fluttered through breathily, "Hello, this is Taeko Tanabe. Is my mother there?"

"No, she isn't, Taeko."

"Thank you," and Taeko hung up before I could say another word. Her voice sounded strange. Mrs. Tanabe was one of

Mother's poet friends. Taeko called three more times, and each time before I could ask her if anything was wrong, she quickly hung up. The next day we learned that Taeko was trying desperately to locate her mother because FBI agents had swept into their home and arrested Mr. Tanabe, a newspaper editor. The FBI had permitted Taeko to try to locate her mother before they took Mr. Tanabe away while they searched the house for contraband and subversive material, but she was not to let anyone else know what was happening.

Next morning the newspapers fairly exploded in our faces with stories about the Japanese raids on the chain of Pacific islands. We were shocked to read Attorney General Biddle's announcement that 736 Japanese had been picked up in the United States and Hawaii. Then Mrs. Tanabe called Mother about her husband's arrest, and she said at least a hundred others had been taken from our community. Messrs. Okayama, Higashi, Sughira, Mori, Okada—we knew them all.

"But why were they arrested, Papa? They weren't spies, were they?"

Father replied almost curtly, "Of course not! They were probably taken for questioning."

The pressure of war moved in on our little community. The Chinese consul announced that all the Chinese would carry identification cards and wear "China" badges to distinguish them from the Japanese. Then I really felt left standing out in the cold. The government ordered the bank funds of all Japanese nationals frozen. Father could no longer handle financial transactions through his bank accounts, but Henry, fortunately, was of legal age so that business could be negotiated in his name.

In the afternoon President Roosevelt's formal declaration of war against Japan was broadcast throughout the nation. In grave, measured words, he described the attack on Pearl Harbor as shameful, infamous. I writhed involuntarily. I could no more have escaped the stab of self-consciousness than I could have changed my Oriental features.

Monday night a complete blackout was ordered against a possible Japanese air raid on the Puget Sound area. Mother assembled black cloths to cover the windows and set up candles in every room. All radio stations were silenced from seven in the evening till morning, but we gathered around the dead radio anyway, out of sheer habit. We whiled away the evening reading instructions in the newspapers on how to put out incendiary bombs and learning about the best hiding places during bombardments. When the city pulled its switches at blackout hour and plunged us into an ominous dark silence, we went to bed shivering and wondering what tomorrow would bring. All of a sudden there was a wild screech of brakes, followed by the resounding crash of metal slamming into metal. We rushed out on the balcony. In the street below we saw dim shapes of cars piled grotesquely on top of each other, their soft blue headlights staring helplessly up into the sky. Angry men's voices floated up to the house. The men were wearing uniforms and their metal buttons gleamed in the blue lights. Apparently two police cars had collided in the blackout.

Clutching at our bathrobes we lingered there. The damp winter night hung heavy and inert like a wet black veil, and at the bottom of Beacon Hill, we could barely make out the undulating length of Rainier Valley, lying quietly in the somber, brooding silence like a hunted python. A few pinpoints of light pricked the darkness here and there like winking bits of diamonds, betraying the uneasy vigil of a tense city.

It made me positively hivey the way the FBI agents continued their raids into Japanese homes and business places and marched the Issei men away into the old red brick immigration building, systematically and efficiently, as if they were stocking a cellarful of choice bottles of wine. At first we noted that the men arrested were those who had been prominent in community affairs, like Mr. Kato, many times president of the Seattle Japanese Chamber of Commerce, and Mr. Ohashi, the principal of our Japanese language school, or individuals whose business was directly connected with firms in Japan; but as time went on, it become less and less apparent why the others were included in these raids.

We wondered when Father's time would come. We expected momentarily to hear strange footsteps on the porch and the sudden demanding ring of the front doorbell. Our ears became attuned like the sensitive antennas of moths, translating every soft swish of passing cars into the arrival of the FBI squad.

Once when our doorbell rang after curfew hour, I completely lost my Oriental stoicism which I had believed would serve me well under the most trying circumstances. No friend of ours paid visits at night anymore, and I was sure that Father's hour had come. As if hypnotized, I walked woodenly to the door. A mass of black figures stood before me, filling the doorway. I let out a magnificent shriek. Then pandemonium broke loose. The solid rank fell apart into a dozen separate figures which stumbled and leaped pell-mell away from the porch. Watching the mad scramble, I thought I had routed the FBI agents with my cry of distress. Father, Mother, Henry, and Sumi rushed out to support my wilting body. When Henry snapped on the porch light, one lone figure crept out from behind the front hedge. It was a newsboy who, standing at a safe distance, called in a quavering voice, "I . . . I came to collect for . . . for the *Times.*"

Shaking with laughter, Henry paid him and gave him an extra large tip for the terrible fright he and his bodyguards had suffered at the hands of the Japanese. As he hurried down the walk, boys of all shapes and sizes crawled out from behind trees and bushes and scurried after him.

We heard all kinds of stories about the FBI, most of them from Mr. Yorita, the grocer, who now took twice as long to make his deliveries. The war seemed to have brought out his personality. At least he talked more, and he glowed, in a sinister way. Before the war Mr. Yorita had been uncommunicative. He used to stagger silently through the back door with a huge sack of rice over his shoulders, dump it on the kitchen floor and silently flow out of the door as if he were bored and disgusted with food and the people who ate it. But now Mr. Yorita swaggered in, sent a gallon jug of soy sauce spinning into a corner, and launched into a comprehensive report of the latest rumors he had picked up on his route, all in chronological order. Mr. Yorita looked like an Oriental Dracula, with his triangular eyes and yellow-fanged teeth. He had a mournfully long sallow face and in his excitement his gold-rimmed glasses constantly slipped to the tip of his long nose. He would describe in detail how some man had been awakened in the dead of night, swiftly handcuffed, and dragged from out of his bed by a squad of brutal, tight-lipped men. Mr. Yorita bared his teeth menacingly in his most dramatic moments, and we shrank from him instinctively. As he backed out of the kitchen door, he would shake his bony finger at us with a warning of dire things to come. When Mother said, "Yorita-san, you must worry about getting a call from the FBI, too," Mr. Yorita laughed modestly, pushing his glasses back up into place. "They wouldn't be interested in anyone as insignificant as myself!" he assured her.

But he was wrong. The following week a new delivery boy appeared at the back door with an airy explanation, "Yep, they got the old man, too, and don't ask me why! The way I see it, it's subversive to sell soy sauce now."

The Matsuis were visited, too. Shortly after Dick had gone to Japan. Mr. Matsui had died and Mrs. Matsui had sold her house. Now she and her daughter and youngest son lived in the back of their little dry goods store on Jackson Street. One day when Mrs. Matsui was busy with the family laundry, three men entered the shop, nearly ripping off the tiny bell hanging over the door. She hurried out, wiping sudsy, reddened hands on her apron. At best Mrs. Matsui's English was rudimentary, and when she became excited, it deteriorated into Japanese. She hovered on her toes, delighted to see new customers in her humble shop. "Yes, yes, something you want?"

"Where's Mr. Matsui?" a steely-eyed man snapped at her.

Startled, Mrs. Matsui jerked her thumb toward the rear of the store and said, "He not home."

"What? Oh, in there, eh? Come on!" The men tore the faded print curtain aside and rushed into the back room. "Don't see him. Must be hiding."

They jerked open bedroom doors, leaped into the tiny bathroom, flung windows open and peered down into the alley. Tiny birdlike Mrs. Matsui rushed around after them. "No, no! Whatsamalla, whatsamalla!"

"Where's your husband! Where is he?" one man demanded angrily, flinging clothes out of the closet.

"Why you mix 'em all up? He not home, not home." She clawed at the back of the burly men like an angry little sparrow, trying to stop the holocaust in her little home. One man brought his face down close to hers, shouting slowly and clearly, "WHERE IS YOUR HUSBAND? YOU SAID HE WAS IN HERE A MINUTE AGO!"

"Yes, yes, not here. *Mah, wakara nai hito da neh.* Such stupid men."

Mrs. Matsui dived under a table, dragged out a huge album, and pointed at a large photograph. She jabbed her gnarled finger up toward the ceiling saying, "Heben! Heben!"

The men gathered around and looked at a picture of Mr. Matsui's funeral. Mrs. Matsui and her two children were standing by a coffin, their eyes cast down, surrounded by all their friends, all of whom were looking down. The three men's lips formed an "Oh." One of them said, "We're sorry to have disturbed you. Thank you, Mrs. Matsui, and good-bye." They departed quickly and quietly.

Having passed through this baptism, Mrs. Matsui became an expert on the FBI, and she stood by us, rallying and coaching us on how to deal with them. She said to Mother, "You must destroy everything and anything Japanese which may incriminate your husband. It doesn't matter what it is, if it's printed or made in Japan, destroy it because the FBI always carries off those items for evidence."

In fact all the women whose husbands had been spirited away said the same thing. Gradually we became uncomfortable with our Japanese books, magazines, wall scrolls, and knickknacks. When Father's hotel friends, Messrs. Sakaguchi, Horiuchi, Nishibue, and a few others vanished, and their wives called Mother weeping and warning her again about having too many Japanese objects around the house, we finally decided to get rid of some of ours. We knew it was impossible to destroy everything. The FBI would certainly think it strange if they found us sitting in a bare house, totally purged of things Japanese. But it was as if we could no longer stand the tension of waiting, and we just had to do something against the black day. We worked all night, feverishly combing through bookshelves, closets, drawers, and furtively creeping down to the basement furnace for the burning. I gathered together my well-worn Japanese language schoolbooks which I had been saving over a period of ten years with the thought that they might come in handy when I wanted to teach Japanese to my own children. I threw them into the fire and watched them flame and shrivel into black ashes. But when I came face to face with my Japanese doll which Grandmother Nagashima had sent me from Japan, I rebelled. It was a gorgeously costumed Miyazukai figure, typical of the lady in waiting who lived in the royal palace during the feudal era. The doll was gowned in an elegant purple silk kimono with the long, sweeping hemline of its period and sashed with rich-embroidered gold and silver brocade. With its black, shining coiffed head bent a little to one side, its delicate pink-tipped ivory hand holding a red lacquer message box, the doll had an appealing, almost human charm. I decided to ask Chris if she would keep it for me. Chris loved and appreciated beauty in every form and shape, and I knew that in her hands, the doll would be safe and enjoyed.

Henry pulled down from his bedroom wall the toy samurai sword he had brought from Japan and tossed it into the flames. Sumi's contributions to the furnace were books of fairy tales and magazines sent to her by her young cousins in Japan. We sorted out Japanese classic and popular music from a stack of records, shattered them over our knees and fed the pieces to the furnace. Father picked up his translated Japanese volumes of philosophy and religion and carted them reluctantly to the basement. Mother had the most to eliminate, with her scrapbooks of poems cut out from newspapers and magazines, and her private collection of old Japanese classic literature.

It was past midnight when we finally climbed upstairs to bed. Wearily we closed our eyes, filled with an indescribable sense of guilt for having destroyed the things we loved. This night of ravage was to haunt us for years. As I lay struggling to fall asleep, I realized that we hadn't freed ourselves at all from fear. We still lay stiff in our beds, waiting.

Mrs. Matsui kept assuring us that the FBI would get around to us yet. It was just a matter of time and the least Mother could do for Father was to pack a suitcase for him. She said that the men captured who hadn't been prepared had grown long beards, lived and slept in the same clothes for days before they were permitted visits from their families. So Mother dutifully packed a suitcase for Father with toilet articles, warm flannel pajamas, and extra clothes, and placed it in the front hall by the door. It was a personal affront, the way it stood there so frank and unabashedly. Henry and I said that it was practically a confession that Papa was a spy, "So please help yourself to him, Mr. FBI, and God speed you."

Mother was equally loud and firm, "No, don't anyone move it! No one thought that Mr. Kato or the others would be taken, but they're gone now. Why should we think Papa's going to be an exception."

Henry threw his hands up in the air and muttered about the odd ways of the Japanese.

Every day Mrs. Matsui called Mother to check Father in; then we caught the habit and started calling him at the hotel every hour on the hour until he finally exploded, "Stop this nonsense! I don't know which is more nerve-wracking, being watched by the FBI or by my family!"

When Father returned home from work, a solicitous family eased him into his favorite armchair, arranged pillows behind his back, and brought the evening paper and slippers to him, Mother cooked Father's favorite dishes frenziedly, night after night. It all made Father very uneasy.

We had a family conference to discuss the possibility of Father and Mother's internment. Henry was in graduate school and I was beginning my second year at the university. We agreed to drop out should they be taken and we would manage the hotel during our parents' absence. Every weekend Henry and I accompanied Father to the hotel and learned how to keep the hotel books, how to open the office safe, and what kind of linen, paper towels, and soap to order.

Then a new menace appeared on the scene. Cries began to sound up and down the coast that everyone of Japanese ancestry should be taken into custody. For years the professional guardians of the Golden West had wanted to rid their land of the Yellow Peril, and the war provided an opportunity for them to push their program through. As the chain of Pacific islands fell to the Japanese, patriots shrieked for protection from us. A Californian sounded the alarm: "The Japanese are dangerous and they must leave. Remember the destruction and the sabotage perpetrated at Pearl Harbor. Notice how they have infiltrated into the harbor towns and taken our best land."

He and his kind refused to be comforted by Edgar Hoover's special report to the War Department stating that there had not been a single case of sabotage committed by a Japanese living in Hawaii or on the mainland during the Pearl Harbor attack or after. I began to feel acutely uncomfortable for living on Beacon Hill. The Marine Hospital rose tall and handsome on our hill, and if I stood on the west shoulder of the Hill, I could not help but get an easily photographed view of the Puget Sound Harbor with its ships snuggled against the docks. And Boeing airfield, a few miles south of us, which had never bothered me before, suddenly seemed to have moved right up into my back yard, daring me to take just one spying glance at it.

In February, Executive Order No. 9066 came out, authorizing the War Department to remove the Japanese from such military areas as it saw fit, aliens and citizens alike. Even if a person had a fraction of Japanese blood in him, he must leave on demand.

A pall of gloom settled upon our home. We couldn't believe that the government meant that the Japanese-Americans must go, too. We had heard the clamoring of superpatriots who insisted loudly, "Throw the whole kaboodle out. A Jap's a Jap, no matter how you slice him. You can't make an American out of little Jap Junior just by handing him an American birth certificate." But we had dismissed these remarks as just hot blasts of air from an overheated patriot. We were quite sure that our rights as American citizens would not be violated, and we would not be marched out of our homes on the same basis as enemy aliens.

In anger, Henry and I read and reread the Executive Order. Henry crumpled the newspaper in his hand and threw it against the wall. "Doesn't my citizenship mean a single blessed thing to anyone? Why doesn't somebody make up my mind for me. First they want me in the army. Now they're going to slap an alien 4-C on me because of my ancestry. What the hell!"

Once more I felt like a despised, pathetic two-headed freak, a Japanese and an American, neither of which seemed to be doing me any good. The Nisei leaders in the community rose above their personal feelings and stated that they would cooperate and comply with the decision of the government as their sacrifice in keeping with the country's war effort, thus proving themselves loyal American citizens. I was too jealous of my recently acquired voting privilege to be gracious about giving in, and I felt most uncooperative. I noticed wryly that the feelings about the Japanese on the Hawaiian Islands were quite different from those on the West Coast. In Hawaii, a strategic military outpost, the Japanese were regarded as essential to the economy of the island and powerful economic forces fought against their removal. General Delos Emmons, in command of Hawaii at the time, lent his authoritative voice to calm the fears of the people on the island and to prevent chaos and upheaval. General Emmons established martial law, but he did not consider evacuation essential for the security of the island.

On the West Coast, General J. L. DeWitt of the Western Defense Command did not think martial law necessary, but he favored mass evacuation of the Japanese and Nisei. We suspected that pressures from economic and political interests who would profit from such a wholesale evacuation influenced this decision.

Events moved rapidly, General DeWitt marked off western Washington, Oregon, and all of California, and the southern half of Arizona as Military Area No. 1, hallowed ground from which we must remove ourselves as rapidly as possible. Unfortunately we could not simply vanish into thin air, and we had no place to go. We had no relatives in the east we could move in on. All our relatives were sitting with us in the forbidden area, themselves wondering where to go. The neighboring states in the line of exit for the Japanese protested violently at the prospect of any mass invasion. They said, very sensibly, that if the coast didn't want the Japanese hanging around, they didn't either.

A few hardy families in the community liquidated their property, tied suitcases all around their cars, and sallied eastward.

They were greeted by signs in front of store windows, "Open season for Japs!" and "We kill rats and Japs here." On state lines, highway troopers swarmed around the objectionable migrants and turned them back under governor's orders.

General DeWitt must have finally realized that if he insisted on voluntary mass evacuation, hundreds and thousands of us would have wandered back and forth, clogging the highways and pitching tents along the roadside, eating and sleeping in colossal disorder. He suddenly called a halt to voluntary movement, although most of the Japanese were not budging an inch. He issued a new order, stating that no Japanese could leave the city, under penalty of arrest. The command had hatched another plan, a better one. The army would move us out as only the army could do it, and march us in neat, orderly fashion into assembly centers. We would stay in these centers only until permanent camps were set up inland to isolate us.

The orders were simple:

Dispose of your homes and property. Wind up your business. Register the family. One seabag of bedding, two suitcases of clothing allowed per person. People in District #1 must report at 8th and Lane Street, 8 P.M. on April 28.

I wanted no part of this new order. I had read in the paper that the Japanese from the state of Washington would be taken to a camp in Puyallup, on the state fairgrounds. The article apologetically assured the public that the camp would be temporary and that the Japanese would be removed from the fairgrounds and parking lots in time for the opening of the annual State Fair. It neglected to say where we might be at the time when those fine breeds of Holstein cattle and Yorkshire hogs would be proudly wearing their blue satin ribbons.

We were advised to pack warm, durable clothes. In my mind, I saw our permanent camp sprawled out somewhere deep in a snow-bound forest, an American Siberia. I saw myself plunging chest deep in the snow, hunting for small game to keep us alive. I decided that one of my suitcases was going to hold nothing but vitamins from A to Z. I thought of sewing fur-lined hoods and parkas for the family. I was certain this was going to be a case of sheer animal survival.

One evening Father told us that he would lose the management of the hotel unless he could find someone to operate it for the duration, someone intelligent and efficient enough to impress Bentley Agent and Company. Father said, "Sam, Joe, Peter, they all promised to stay on their jobs, but none of them can read or write well enough to manage the business. I've got to find a responsible party with experience in hotel management, but where?"

Sumi asked, "What happens if we can't find anyone?"

"I lose my business and my livelihood. I'll be saying good-bye to a lifetime of labor and all the hopes and plans I had for the family."

We sagged. Father looked at us thoughtfully, "I've never talked much about the hotel business to you children, mainly because so much of it has been an uphill climb of work and waiting for better times. Only recently I was able to clear up the loans I took out years ago to expand the business. I was sure that in the next five or ten years I would be getting returns on my long-range investments, and I would have been able to do a lot of things eventually. . . . Send you through medical school," Father nodded to Henry, "and let Kazu and Sumi study anything they liked." Father laughed a bit self-consciously as he looked at Mother, "And when all the children had gone off on their own, I had planned to take Mama on her first real vacation, to Europe as well as Japan."

We listened to Father wide-eyed and wistful. It had been a wonderful, wonderful dream.

Mother suddenly hit upon a brilliant idea. She said maybe the Olsens, our old friends who had once managed the Camden Apartments might be willing to run a hotel. The Olsens had sold the apartment and moved to Aberdeen. Mother thought that perhaps Marta's oldest brother, the bachelor of the family, might be available. If he refused, perhaps Marta and her husband might consider the offer. We rushed excitedly to the telephone to make a long-distance call to the Olsens. After four wrong Olsens, we finally reached Marta.

"Marta? Is this Marta?"

"Yes, this is Marta."

I nearly dove into the mouthpiece, I was so glad to hear her voice. Marta remembered us well and we exchanged news about our families. Marta and her husband had bought a small chicken farm and were doing well. Marta said, "I come from the farm ven I vas young and I like it fine. I feel more like home here. How's everybody over there?"

I told her that we and all the rest of the Japanese were leaving Seattle soon under government order on account of the war. Marta gasped, "Everybody? You mean the Saitos, the Fujinos, Watanabes, and all the rest who were living at the Camden Apartments, too?"

"Yes, they and everyone else on the West Coast."

Bewildered, Marta asked where we were going, what we were going to do, would we ever return to Seattle, and what about Father's hotel. I told her about our business situation and that Father needed a hotel manager for the duration. Would she or any of her brothers be willing to accept such a job? There was a silence at the other end of the line and I said hastily, "This is a very sudden call, Marta. I'm sorry I had to surprise you like this, but we felt this was an emergency and . . ."

Marta was full of regrets, "Oh, I vish we could do something to help you folks, but my husband and I can't leave the farm at all. We don't have anyone here to help. We do all the work ourselves. Magnus went to Alaska last year. He has a goot job up there, some kind of war work. My other two brothers have business in town and they have children so they can't help you much."

My heart sank like a broken elevator. When I said, "Oh . . ." I felt the family sitting behind me sink into a gloomy silence. Our last hope was gone. We finally said good-bye, Marta distressed at not being able to help, and I apologizing for trying to hoist our problem on them.

The next weekend Marta and Karl paid us a surprise visit. We had not seen them for nearly two years. Marta explained shyly, "It was such a nice day and we don't go novair for a long time, so I tole Karl, 'Let's take a bus into Seattle and visit the Itois.'"

We spent a delightful Sunday afternoon talking about old times. Mother served our guests her best green tea and, as we relaxed, the irritating presence of war vanished. When it was time for them to return home, Marta's sparkling blue eyes suddenly filled, "Karl and I, we feel so bad about the whole ting, the war and everything, we joost had to come out to see you, and say 'good-bye.' God bless you. Maybe we vill see you again back home here. Anyvay, we pray for it."

Marta and Karl's warmth and sincerity restored a sense of peace into our home, an atmosphere which had disappeared ever since Pearl Harbor. They served to remind us that in spite of the bitterness war had brought into our lives, we were still bound to our hometown. Bit by bit, I remembered our happy

past, the fun we had growing up along the colorful brash waterfront, swimming through the white-laced waves of Puget Sound,
and lolling luxuriously on the tender green carpet of grass
around Lake Washington from where we could see the slick,
blue-frosted shoulders of Mount Rainier. There was too much
beauty surrounding us. Above all, we must keep friends like
Marta and Karl, Christine, Sam, Peter and Joe, all sterling prod-
ucts of many years of associations. We could never turn our
faces away and remain aloof forever from Seattle.

Fish Cheeks

Amy Tan

I fell in love with the minister's son the winter I turned four-teen. He was not Chinese, but as white as Mary in the manger. For Christmas I prayed for this blond-haired boy, Robert, and a slim new American nose.

When I found out that my parents had invited the minister's family over for Christmas Eve dinner, I cried. What would Robert think of our shabby *Chinese* Christmas? What would he think of our noisy *Chinese* relatives who lacked proper American manners? What terrible disappointment would he feel upon seeing not a roasted turkey and sweet potatoes but *Chinese* food?

On Christmas Eve I saw that my mother had outdone herself in creating a strange menu. She was pulling black veins out of the backs of fleshy prawns. The kitchen was littered with appalling mounds of raw food: A slimy rock cod with bulging fish eyes that pleaded not to be thrown into a pan of hot oil. Tofu, which looked like stacked wedges of rubbery white sponges. A bowl soaking dried fungus back to life. A plate of squid, their backs crisscrossed with knife markings so they resembled bicycle tires.

And then they arrived—the minister's family and all my relatives in a clamor of doorbells and rumpled Christmas packages. Robert grunted hello, and I pretended he was not worthy of existence.

Dinner threw me deeper into despair. My relatives licked the ends of their chopsticks and reached across the table, dipping them into the dozen or so plates of food. Robert and his family waited patiently for platters to be passed to them. My relatives murmured with pleasure when my mother brought out the whole steamed fish. Robert grimaced. Then my father poked his chopsticks just below the fish eye and plucked out the soft meat. "Amy, your favorite," he said, offering me the tender fish cheek. I wanted to disappear.

At the end of the meal my father leaned back and belched loudly, thanking my mother for her fine cooking. "It's a polite Chinese custom to show you are satisfied," explained my father to our astonished guests. Robert was looking down at his plate with a reddened face. The minister managed to muster up a quiet burp. I was stunned into silence for the rest of the night.

After everyone had gone, my mother said to me, "You want to be the same as American girls on the outside." She handed me an early gift. It was a miniskirt in beige tweed. "But inside you must always be Chinese. You must be proud you are different. Your only shame is to have shame."

And even though I didn't agree with her then, I knew that she understood how much I had suffered during the evening's dinner. It wasn't until many years later—long after I had gotten over my crush on Robert—that I was able to fully appreciate her lesson and the true purpose behind our particular menu. For Christmas Eve that year, she had chosen all my favorite foods.

Lucky to Be Born a Chinese

Jade Snow Wong

THE months filled with schoolwork, music lessons, and home chores were broken in routine by a few days which glowed. These were the seven days of the Chinese New Year. According to the Chinese lunar calendar, New Year's fell in the American February, unless it was a Chinese "leap year," which gave the year an extra seventh month. These holidays climaxed the year and the American-Chinese children at public school were excused for their festivities.

. . . The Wong children, all scrubbed and with their hair washed, were dressed in new clothes, for New Year's literally meant that everything should be new, renewed, or clean. The children also tried to be very good, for a scolding on New Year's day foretokened frequent scoldings during the year. It was also poor taste to talk about unpleasant subjects, such as death, for that would also bring bad luck; therefore visitors uttered the most flattering remarks and offered exaggerated good wishes, such as, "May you be blessed with a hundred sons and a thousand grandsons!" or "May you enjoy the best of health and longevity!" or "May you find your great material fortune this year!"

The sidewalks on both sides of Grant Avenue were lined with colorful exhibits when "The New Year's Thirtieth Night" or New Year's Eve approached. Huge branches from blossoming trees, such as the peach, pear, or apricot, were placed beside open-tiered shelves laden with pots of flowering azaleas, camellias, gardenias, cyclamen, and early-budding bulbs of narcissus and daffodils. Because of its delicacy and heavenly fragrance the traditional narcissus bulb with double blossoms, which grew in water, was always the favorite. . . .

Mama took Jade Snow and Jade Precious Stone and Forgiveness from Heaven through the streets to see all the sights, for although Mama would not leave the house the year 'round, on "The Year's Thirtieth Night" it was her privilege and desire to go out and enjoy the community gaiety for one evening.

The streets, narrow to begin with, were now made even narrower by the displays; they were also jammed by shoppers looking for choice purchases. The busy hum of the crowd and the merchants' cries created an undercurrent of excitement. A festive spirit flowed from the well-dressed children and their dressed-up mothers, all seemingly relaxed and carefree in their holiday mood and costumes.

Mama did not buy anything; she had her hands occupied with Forgiveness and Jade Precious Stone. Besides, Daddy had already bought all their groceries for their wonderful New Year's meals—one feast tonight for "Rounding Out the Year" and one day after tomorrow to "Open the Year."

On New Year's Eve, when they got home, they discovered that Daddy had gone out too by himself and had brought back a huge branch of pink blossoms, which now graced their one and only antique vase, a handsome black porcelain piece with a colorful dragon decoration. The faint perfume of almond blossoms pervaded their dining room. . . .

The Wongs expected callers every day of the New Year week, and they were prepared not only with a spotless home but also with decorations of bright oranges and tangerines neatly stacked on plates, new potted plants, and red hangings and pillow covers.

Jade Snow helped Mama pass sweetmeats and red melon seeds to their guests. The sweetmeats were candied melon, coconut, or kumquats, and lichee nuts from China. The red melon seeds were consumed by the visitors with remarkable skill. They cracked the tiny kernel's outer shell with their teeth, and extracted the thin white seed expertly without breaking it, continuing this tirelessly all afternoon without interrupting their conversation. (In a Chinese gathering melon seeds took the place of cigarettes; and during visits, at the theater, and at banquets, the click, click, click of cracking shells always told of a sociable occasion.) The red and green colors, the fruit, the green plants, the flowering branches, the seeds, the sweets—all were propitious: they meant life, new life, a fruitful life, and a sweet life.

During New Year's, Chinese women worked at jobs irregularly or not at all; the most important thing was to celebrate properly. The women who were regularly employees of Daddy's visited his home as guests. There were many exchanges of sweets, and Jade Snow was never hungry during that week. In addition, callers tucked into the children's hands at least a quarter and sometimes fifty cents or a silver dollar, wrapped in red paper for a good-luck token of material wealth during the year. Mama reciprocated by giving the callers' children similar good-luck packets. Some of Jade Snow's schoolmates returned to class with tales of the amount of gift money they had kept for themselves, but she always had to give hers back to Mama.

The delicious tidbits exchanged at New Year's varied according to the pride and custom of individual households. Some prided themselves on steamed sweet puddings, made of brown sugar and special flours, and decorated with red dates or sesame seeds. Others specialized in salty puddings, made with ground-root flour (something like potato flour), fat pork, chopped baby shrimps, mushrooms, red ginger, and green-topped with parsley (baby coriander leaves). Some families brought a special deep-fried dumpling filled with ground soybeans and rolled in sesame seeds, to be eaten piping hot. Still other women spent considerable time in making tiny turnovers which consisted of a delectable filling of chopped roast pork, bamboo shoots, and spices, rolled in a thin, chewy, translucent paste, and steamed on bamboo racks. . . .

At the Wongs', the New Year week got a good start at the "Opening of the Year" with an extra-bountiful dinner which featured Daddy's special chicken dish and a huge roast duck. The celebration also had a good wind-up on its seventh and last day called "The Day Man Was Made," with another feast. Of course, the dinner did not end with chicken or duck; there were special dried-vegetable-and-oyster stews and other time-consuming dishes which were not usually served.

To "Open the Year," Daddy—who cooked only when he was enormously pleased with the occasion—usually fixed his lichee chicken. . . .

During the week that followed, there were Lion Dances daily on the streets. Daddy took them to watch the dancing, now holding Forgiveness high on his shoulder, to watch the performance from unobstructed heights. It was the custom in San Francisco for the Chinese hospital to raise its yearly funds by engaging a "lion" to dance for his money. A group of acrobats trained in the technique relieved one another in these dances. They used a large and ferocious-looking but very colorful "lion's head," fitted with bright eyes on springs, and a jaw on hinges. From this head there hung a fancy satin "body" and "tail" piece, sewn together with different-colored scalloped strips of coral, turquoise, red, green, and blue silk. One man who set the tempo for the dance manipulated the head, holding it up in both hands, with only his brightly trousered and slippered legs showing below. As the huge Chinese drums beat in quickening tempo, he danced hard, raised the head high, and jerked it from side to side in an inquiring and delighted manner. His partner, holding up the tail, danced in accompaniment. Their lively movements simulated the stalking, attack, and retreat of a lion.

Citizens of Chinatown co-operated by hanging red paper tied with currency and lettuce leaves in front of their doorways. The lion approached and danced up to the prize. Sometimes, he had to dance onto a stool to reach it. As he stretched his hand out through the mouth to grab the money, his feet keeping time on the stool all the while, the occupant of the house or store threw out strings of bursting firecrackers, both to welcome him and to scare away the evil spirits. Daddy, with Jade Snow, Jade Precious Stone, and Forgiveness from Heaven, followed the lion's trail, treading the red fragments of burnt firecracker wrappings which carpeted the gray sidewalks.

Jade Snow was always fascinated by the Lion Dance—the insistent strong beat of the drums was exhilarating, and the colors and rhythm were unforgettable. But sometimes she felt sorry for the lion, especially when it was hot, or when the bursting firecrackers were thrown right at the "fearless" animal.

The firecrackers were set off to frighten away any lingering evil spirits, and to make the New Year fresh and clean. They came from China and were of various sizes. The tiny ones were hardly worth burning, and were useful to pack with stored clothing to keep away moths. The next size was most popular. In a continuous string they made a great deal of noise, and singly they were still effective. . . . There were still bigger ones which Jade Snow was not allowed to burn. These were called "big lights" and could blow up a bottle or lift a tin can. . . .

Another festival which was traditional with the Chinese and therefore with the Wong family was the Moon Festival.

As long as Jade Snow could remember, their family had unfailingly and appropriately observed the holiday, which was said to have originated in ancient China. According to the Chinese lunar calendar, on the fifteenth day of the eighth month the moon would rise rounder, larger, and more brightly golden than at any other month of the year. Then, specially baked cakes filled with a thick, sweet filling were eaten by the Chinese in recognition of the beautiful, full harvest moon. The round Chinatown moon cakes which Jade Snow knew were about four inches in diameter and an inch and a half thick. Thin, short, sweet golden pastry was wrapped around rich fillings of ground lotus pods, or candied coconut and melon, or ground sweetened soybean paste. Jade Snow's favorite filling was "five seeds." This was a crunchy, sweet, nutty mixture of lotus pods, almonds, melon seeds, olive seeds, and sesame seeds. Each cake was cut into small wedges, to be enjoyed slowly with tea. Daddy always said that his father in China used to be able to cut his cake into sixteen to thirty-two wedges; one cake would last him all afternoon as he sat on his front porch to eat and drink and leisurely watch the rest of the village go by his door.

At Moon Festival time, Grandfather also called for a special rice-soup dinner for a large crowd of friends and employees. . . . A rice-soup dinner was informal and a social occasion for fun.

Yes, it was sometimes very lucky to be born a Chinese daughter. The Americans, Jade Snow heard, did not have a Moon Festival nor a seven-day New Year celebration with delicious accompaniments. Besides, they burned their Chinese firecrackers five months later on one day only—the Fourth of July!

Foreign Ways

Diana Chang

If I were in China this minute
and running after a friend
spied across from the hotel
I was staying at

waving to him, say
calling his name in Mandarin

Still they'd know me—
the body giving the person away
betrays a mind
of its own—

my voice from Duluth
my lope with its prairie air

Saying Yes

Diana Chang

"Are you Chinese?"
"Yes."

"American?"
"Yes."

"*Really* Chinese?"
"No . . . not quite."

"*Really* American?"
"Well, actually, you see . . ."

But I would rather say
yes

Not neither-nor,
not maybe,
but both, and not only

The homes I've had,
the ways I am

I'd rather say it
twice,
yes

The Floral Apron

Marilyn Chin

The woman wore a floral apron around her neck,
that woman from my mother's village
with a sharp cleaver in her hand.
She said, "What shall we cook tonight?
Perhaps these six tiny squid
lined up so perfectly on the block?"

She wiped her hand on the apron,
pierced the blade into the first.
There was no resistance,
no blood, only cartilage
soft as a child's nose. A last
iota of ink made us wince.

Suddenly, the aroma of ginger and scallion fogged our
    senses,
and we absolved her for that moment's barbarism.
Then, she, an elder of the tribe,
without formal headdress, without elegance,
deigned to teach the younger
about the Asian plight.

And although we have traveled far
we would never forget that primal lesson
—on patience, courage, forbearance,
on how to love squid despite squid,
how to honor the village, the tribe,
that floral apron.

from

Songs of Gold Mountain

Marlon K. Hom, Editor

Immigration Blues

THE Chinese Exclusion Act of 1882 opened an infamous chapter in United States immigration history, one that brought insurmountable hardship to the Chinese. The moment that their ship docked at the San Francisco pier, the Chinese immigrants were herded into the notorious detention center known to all the Chinese as the "Muk uk" (Mu wu), or "Wooden Barracks," to be processed for immigration. Before 1910, detainees were sent to a wooden building alongside the Pacific Mail Steamship Company pier that was known as the "Tongsaan Matau" (Tangshan Matou), the China Dock (now Pier 50 on the San Francisco waterfront). Because of rampant corruption and the facility's poor physical condition, it ceased to be used in 1910. Instead, the government put into operation the newly built Angel Island Immigration Station in San Francisco Bay to process immigrants and returnees from Asia. This station was sometimes called the Ellis Island of the West Coast.

At Angel Island, the Chinese had to submit to a battery of physical examinations and harsh interrogations. Those who passed were ferried to San Francisco to begin their new life; those who did not were deported back to China permanently. Detainees at the Wooden Barracks were not allowed to go beyond the compound or to meet any outside visitors. It was not uncommon to be detained in the Wooden Barracks for several weeks, even over a year, while awaiting processing: The facilities were minimal, without any consideration for privacy. Suicides were not unknown.

Many of the Chinese at the Angel Island Wooden Barracks wrote poems expressing their agony, frustration, anger, and despair. They would scribble the lines all over the walls of the barracks where they slept. In the 1930s, two detainees copied these scribbles and brought them to San Francisco. However, this genre of Chinese immigration poetry remained unknown to most people until recently.

In 1940, a fire destroyed the administration building of the

Angel Island Immigration Station, and the use of the facility was soon halted. Detainees were moved to another detention center in San Francisco. Barrack 37, the housing compound, survived the fire, but was forgotten for thirty years. Finally in the early 1970s, when the building was targeted for demolition, the Chinese scribbles on the walls caught the attention of the Chinese in San Francisco. Community efforts from Chinatown saved Barrack 37, and it has since become a historical site, augmented by an exhibit on the island's Chinese immigration history. Over 135 Wooden Barracks poems are extant today.

The Cantonese folk rhymes on immigration in the 1911 anthology represent the earliest collection of published poems dealing with the Chinese immigration experience. They are different from the poems on the Wooden Barracks walls. Not only do these rhymes protest the harsh treatment at the Wooden Barracks; they also show that Angel Island with its Wooden Barracks was not a euphoric Ellis Island for the Chinese immigrants. Instead, it was a contradiction of the principles of liberty that testified to injustice. The criticism, so pronounced in the rhymes, reveals that the Chinese immigrants did have an appreciation of the American principles of justice and democracy. They expected to be treated on that level and they believed that they should be accorded such rights. This was, I believe, the first crude sign of their Americanization.

1

As soon as it is announced
    the ship has reached America:
I burst out cheering,
    I have found precious pearls.
How can I bear the detention upon arrival,
Doctors and immigration officials refusing
    to let me go?
All the abuse—
I can't describe it with a pen.
I'm held captive in a wooden barrack, like King Wen
    in Youli:
No end to the misery and sadness in my heart.

2

The moment I hear
    we've entered the port,
I am all ready:
    my belongings wrapped in a bundle.
Who would have expected joy to become sorrow:
Detained in a dark, crude, filthy room?
What can I do?
Cruel treatment, not one restful breath of air.
Scarcity of food, severe restrictions—all
    unbearable.
Here even a proud man bows his head low.

3

In search of a pin-head gain,
I was idle in an impoverished village.
I've risked a perilous journey to come to the Flowery
     Flag Nation.
Immigration officers interrogated me;
And, just for a slight lapse of memory,
I am deported, and imprisoned in this barren
     mountain.
A brave man cannot use his might here,
And he can't take one step beyond the confines.

4

At home I was in poverty,
     constantly worried about firewood and rice,
I borrowed money
     to come to Gold Mountain.
Immigration officers cross-examined me;
     no way could I get through.
Deported to this island,
     like a convicted criminal.
Here—
Mournful sighs fill the gloomy room.
A nation weak; her people often humiliated
Like animals, tortured and destroyed at others'
     whim.

5

Wooden barracks, all specially built;
It's clear they're detention cells.
We Chinese enter this country and suffer
All sorts of autocratic restrictions made at
    whim.
What a disappointment—
Cooped up inside an iron cage;
We have an impotent ambassador who cannot
    handle matters.
We knit our brows and cry for heaven gives no
    recourse for our suffering.

7

Detention is called "awaiting review."
No letter or message can get through to me.
My mind's bogged down with a hundred frustrations
    and anxieties,
My mouth balks at meager meals of rice gruel.
O, what can I do?
Just when can I go ashore?
Imprisoned in a coop, unable to breathe,
My countrymen are made into a herd of cattle!

Lamentations of Stranded Sojourners

ECONOMIC hardship is the theme of the rhymes contained in this section. In recruiting Cantonese to work as laborers in America's West, Western capitalists preached the promise and glory of economic advancement. The possibility of attaining a better life was an irresistible temptation in southeastern China during the mid-nineteenth century, as many of the inhabitants of the region had been reduced to a marginal existence by natural and human disasters. Therefore, the news of economic opportunity was a welcome relief, and the discovery of gold in California only further encouraged the desperate Cantonese natives to rush to the United States. The promise of a steady income by working on the construction of the transcontinental railroads was also readily accepted by the impoverished men. Thus, they made the journey, thousands of miles across the perilous Pacific Ocean, pursuing their Gold Mountain Dream of success, a dream not too different from that of their European immigrant counterparts.

The Chinese immigrants worked hard at their jobs. They reclaimed California land and laid the foundation for the state to become the salad bowl of America. They mined claims that had been abandoned by white miners, paying a hefty foreign miners' tax. They worked on railroad construction, handling the most dangerous assignments, at a cost of thousands of lives. The wages they were paid, however, were lower than those of white workers. When they struck to demand better pay, their employer cut off their food supplies and the white workers did not support them. In the winter season, they lived and worked literally in the snow while laying track through the Sierra mountains. An avalanche could claim many lives without warning. When spring finally arrived, the bodies would emerge from the melting snow, intact, still holding picks and shovels, as a frozen testimony to their hardships.

Hardship and labor in the United States were an accepted reality for these Cantonese men, but the rampant racial prejudice of American society only made their lives more miserable. Even in urban San Francisco, their economic opportunities were limited. Many became disillusioned upon realizing that, after years of toiling in pain, there was not one sign of relief. Increasing their plight was the agony and frustration that they felt when they recognized the fact that their journey to America was not made just for themselves. Their sense of duty to their families back in China, who depended on them for survival, became an ever-present reminder, pushing them to the edge of desperation. A man's ability to achieve economic success and to provide for his family was the ultimate judgment of his success in the American sojourn. Anything less than that would be considered a failure. Thus, the most poignant reference in these rhymes is not to hardship or physical labor, but to the lack of economic reward. When their labor went unrewarded, many of these men became resigned to fate and disillusioned; others still desperately continued trying. Regardless of their differing responses to this harsh reality, all were haunted by the Gold Mountain Dream.

18

Dispirited by life in my village home,
I make a journey specially to the United States
  of America.
Separated by mountains and passes, I feel an
  extreme anxiety and grief;
Rushing about east and west does me no good.
Turning in all directions—
An ideal opportunity has yet to come.
If fate is indeed Heaven's will, what more can
  I say?
'Tis a disgrace to a man's pride and dignity.

19

Born into a rotten life,
Coming or going, all without leaving my mark.
Even after leaving the village for a foreign
  country,
Running about east and west, I've gained nothing.
Everything's turned upside down;
It's more disconcerting being away from home.
I have gone to the four corners of the world;
Alas, I am neither at ease while resting nor
  happy while moving.

20

Pitiful is the twenty-year sojourner,
Unable to make it home.
Having been everywhere—north, south, east,
  west—
Always obstacles along the way, pain knitting
  my brows.
Worried, in silence.
Ashamed, wishes unfulfilled.
A reflection on the mirror, a sudden fright:
  hair, half frost-white.
Frequent letters from home, all filled with much
  complaint.

21

Come to think of it, what can I really say?
Thirty years living in the United States—
Why has life been so miserable and I, so frail?
I suppose it's useless to expect to go home.
My heart aches with grief;
My soul wanders around aimlessly.
Unable to make a living here, I'll try it in the East,
With a sudden change of luck, I may make it back to
  China.

22

Stranded in a lodge: a delay;
Old debts up to my ears: here to stay.
No sign of relief, only a pain stealing through
  my heart.
And nagged by worry for my aged parents.
I want to go home;
But what can I do without money in my purse?
Determined to shape up and shake loose, I move
  elsewhere;
But I am still stuck with rotten luck, as life only
  gets worse.

23

I have walked to the very ends of the earth,
A dusty, windy journey.
I've toiled and I'm worn out, all for a miserable lot.
Nothing is ideal when I am down and out.
I think about it day and night—
Who can save a fish out of water?
From far away, I worry for my parents, my wife,
  my boy:
Do they still have enough firewood, rice, salt, and
  cooking oil?

The Legend

Garrett Hongo

In Chicago, it is snowing softly
and a man has just done his wash for the week.
He steps into the twilight of early evening,
carrying a wrinkled shopping bag
full of neatly folded clothes,
and, for a moment, enjoys
the feel of warm laundry and crinkled paper,
flannellike against his gloveless hands.
There's a Rembrandt glow on his face,
a triangle of orange in the hollow of his cheek
as a last flash of sunset
blazes the storefronts and lit windows of the street.

He is Asian, Thai or Vietnamese,
and very skinny, dressed as one of the poor
in rumpled suit pants and a plaid mackinaw,
dingy and too large.
He negotiates the slick of ice
on the sidewalk by his car,
opens the Fairlane's back door,
leans to place the laundry in,
and turns, for an instant,
toward the flurry of footsteps
and cries of pedestrians
as a boy—that's all he was—
backs from the corner package store
shooting a pistol, firing it,
once, at the dumbfounded man
who falls forward,
grabbing at his chest.

A few sounds escape from his mouth,
a babbling no one understands
as people surround him
bewildered at his speech.
The noises he makes are nothing to them.
The boy has gone, lost
in the light array of foot traffic
dappling the snow with fresh prints.

Tonight, I read about Descartes'
grand courage to doubt everything
except his own miraculous existence
and I feel so distinct
from the wounded man lying on the concrete
I am ashamed.

Let the night sky cover him as he dies.
Let the weaver girl cross the bridge of heaven
and take up his cold hands.

In Memory of Jay Kashiwamura

What For

Garrett Hongo

At six I lived for spells:
how a few Hawaiian words could call
up the rain, could hymn like the sea
in the long swirl of chambers
curling in the nautilus of a shell,
how Amida's ballads of the Buddhaland
in the drone of the priest's liturgy
could conjure money from the poor
and give them nothing but mantras,
the strange syllables that healed desire.

I lived for stories about the war
my grandfather told over *hana* cards,
slapping them down on the mats
with a sharp Japanese *kiai.*

I lived for songs my grandmother sang
stirring curry into a thick stew,
weaving a calligraphy of Kannon's love
into grass mats and straw sandals.

I lived for the red volcano dirt
staining my toes, the salt residue
of surf and sea wind in my hair,
the arc of a flat stone skipping
in the hollow trough of a wave.

I lived a child's world, waited
for my father to drag himself home,
dusted with blasts of sand, powdered rock,
and the strange ash of raw cement,
his deafness made worse by the clang
of pneumatic drills, sore in his bones
from the buckings of a jackhammer.
He'd hand me a scarred lunchpail,
let me unlace the hightop G.I. boots,
call him the new name I'd invented

that day in school, write it for him
on his newspaper. He'd rub my face
with hands that felt like gravel roads,
tell me to move, go play, and then he'd
walk to the laundry sink to scrub,
rinse the dirt of his long day
from a face brown and grained as koa wood.

I wanted to take away the pain
in his legs, the swelling in his joints,
give him back his hearing,
clear and rare as crystal chimes,
the fins of glass that wrinkled
and sparked the air with their sound.

I wanted to heal the sores that work
and war had sent to him,
let him play catch in the backyard
with me, tossing a tennis ball
past papaya trees without the shoulders
of pain shrugging back his arms.

I wanted to become a doctor of pure magic,
to string a necklace of sweet words
fragrant as pine needles and plumeria,
fragrant as the bread my mother baked,
place it like a lei of cowrie shells
and *pikake* flowers around my father's neck,
and chant him a blessing, a sutra.

Concentration Constellation

Lawson Fusao Inada

In this earthly configuration,
we have, not points of light,
but prominent barbs of dark.

It's all right there on the map.
It's all right there in the mind.
Find it. If you care to look.

Begin between the Golden State's
highest and lowest elevations
and name that location

Manzanar. Rattlesnake a line
southward to the zone
of Arizona, to the home
of natives on the reservation,
and call those Gila, Poston.

Then just take your time
winding your way across
the Southwest expanse, the Lone
Star State of Texas, gathering
up a mess of blues as you
meander around the banks
of the humid Mississippi; yes,
just make yourself at home
in the swamps of Arkansas,
for this is Rohwer and Jerome.

By now, you weary of the way.
It's a big country, you say.
It's a big history, hardly
halfway through—with Amache
looming in the Colorado desert,

Heart Mountain high in wide
Wyoming, *Minidoka* on the moon
of Idaho, then down to Utah's
jewel of *Topaz* before finding
yourself at northern California's
frozen shore of *Tule Lake* . . .

Now regard what sort of shape
this constellation takes.
It sits there like a jagged scar,
massive, on the massive landscape.
It lies there like the rusted wire
of a twisted and remembered fence.

Father of My Father

Lawson Fusao Inada

for Mitsuji Inada

I

The way the incense gripped,
coughing, everyone coughing,
their throats resounding in the hall . . .

Above the stage, a dragon
licked his lip.

They were moaning, bowing and moaning—
three old-kimonoed men,
their tassels flapping.

The altar bristled
lacquer and gold latches.

Then clapping wood, the gift
of incense to the bowl . . .

II

Incense. Sucking the wind from him—
face a deflated callus . . .

Then the shoes paraded, on and on,
issuing from the walls.

Finally, to be strolling
over the garden—

gaunt rocks, bonsai
knuckled at the bottom.

About, all structures
surrounding the pagoda of San Jose.

III

Have you ever seen
blue eyes in a Japanese face?

That is the main thing I remember.

She took the wrong road
nightly at their intersection,
leaving him shouting, screaming,
pacing the house with a flashlight

as if something was missing.

Have you ever lost your woman?
Have you ever lost your crops
and had to move?—
packing up without your woman,
some evacuation going on . . .

Have you ever been wakened
by blue eyes shining into your face?

You wondered who you were.

You couldn't move.

Or there were evenings
steeped in scrolls and incense . . .

Sometimes, to be alone
in that museum, cleaved
by shadows, the tongue's disfigurings . . .

In Arkansas he staked a ragged garden.
Then that Colorado wind
eroded.

I flourished in that sand.

But what comes second-hand
is not the same.

Something is missing.

I sometimes wake to streetlight
pacing in my room.

I would not hold him then.

Nothing could stop me now.

On Being Asian American

Lawson Fusao Inada

for Our Children

Of course, not everyone
can be an Asian American.
Distinctions are earned,
and deserve dedication.

Thus, from time of birth,
the journey awaits you
ventures through time,
the turns of the earth.

When you seem to arrive,
the journey continues;
when you seem to arrive,
the journey continues.

Take me as I am, you cry.
I, I, am an individual.
Which certainly is true.
Which generates an echo.

Who are all your people
assembled in celebration,
with wisdom and strength,
to which you are entitled.

For you are at the head
of succeeding generations,
as the rest of the world
comes forward to greet you.

the promise

Alan Chong Lau

for Sharon Lew and the first, second,
third, and all generations to come . . .
workers of the soil, all children
of the land

1
my grandfather
detained
on an island
of hell named angel

    "from your backdoor
how many feet
is the village pond?
in what direction
does your house
    lie in relation to it?"

      —immigration authority questions
    your parents
    contained
    up here in the *original* tules
    where it still snows
    in april
    streaks of white
    on engulfing crags of stone

    here where man
    is a pin
    and silence replaces the scream
    of anger once righteous enough
    to bring tanks grumbling to
    the barbed front door

    your used barracks
    are rented out to new prisoners

migrant workers
who stoop over to pick
the dark mud from their shoes
as geese draw the distance
between peaks

here on an island
of sun bleached rocks
where chinese grandmothers
sat on benches
in the long afternoon
waiting years feet inches
for entrance to gold mountain
the broken glass of windows
lay on the floor
jagged tears eating dust

green thriving bushes
cover walls where inside
poems of despair
ten thousand washed out dreams
are scrawled in bitter blood
as sea gulls cut white patterns
in blue sky

today we rode in chartered buses
to get here
with scant belongings as
your parents once rode in buses

bayonets at every window
            like a road sign

a former internee
speaks
"this is the first time
i've been here in . . ."

(eyes scan
tarpaper walls
counting up time spent
a collapsed guardtower
points to the mountains)

142

"thirty years . . .
it's been . . ."

(the wind cuts us all
to silence

as he no longer
can find words)

today
i take a ferry
across the water
with only a sack lunch
as my grandfather
carried only a bundle wrapped in cloth
tossed in the hold of a ship
like a wet mop
the words on the walls speak
"deprived of my freedom, i stay on this island.

the story of my life is bleached—ending up
in prison.
my breast is full of grievances and this poem
is an outlet."

2
we come in
all of us with names
not numbers
and

no . . .
we will never
go to tule lake again

and no . . .
i cannot tell you how many feet
the duckpond is from my backdoor

and no . . .
we will never
give up our names

and yes . . .
this land is our land

and yes . . .
we will share it with
people of all tribes

and yes . . .
all your guns
are worthless

and yes . . .
it is the same with your empty words

the earth will eat them
will split them
like pulling off the heads
of rusty nails

Eating Together

Li-Young Lee

In the steamer is the trout
seasoned with slivers of ginger,
two sprigs of green onion, and sesame oil.
We shall eat it with rice for lunch,
brothers, sister, my mother who will
taste the sweetest meat of the head,
holding it between her fingers
deftly, the way my father did
weeks ago. Then he lay down
to sleep like a snow-covered road
winding through pines older than him,
without any travelers, and lonely for no one.

I Ask My Mother to Sing

Li-Young Lee

She begins, and my grandmother joins her.
Mother and daughter sing like young girls.
If my father were alive, he would play
his accordian and sway like a boat.

I've never been in Peking, or the Summer Palace,
nor stood on the great Stone Boat to watch
the rain begin on Kuen Ming Lake, the picnickers
running away from the grass.

But I love to hear it sung:
how the waterlilies fill with rain until
they overturn, spilling water into water,
then rock back, and fill with more.

Both women have begun to cry.
But neither stops her song.

Father From Asia

Shirley Geok-lin Lim

Father, you turn your hands toward me.
Large hollow bowls, they are empty
stigmata of poverty. Light pours
through them, and I back away,
for you are dangerous, father
of poverty, father of ten children,
father of nothing, from whose life
I have learned nothing for myself.
You are the father of childhood,
father from Asia, father of sacrifice.
I renounce you, keep you in my sleep,
keep you two oceans away, ghost
who eats his own children,
Asia who loved his children,
who didn't know abandonment,
father who lived at the center of the world,
whose life I dare not remember,
for memory is a wheel that crushes,
and Asia is dust, is dust.

Deciding

Tran Thi Nga and Wendy Wilder Larsen

We went to the office every day.
Though the situation was critical,
people at work said nothing.
Province Chiefs were running.
We told the Big Boss our country would be lost.
We told him we would blow ourselves up
if we could not leave.

I sat at my desk doing the financial report.
My thoughts went round and round.

Should I leave?
Should I go alone?
Should I take my mother?
She did not want to go.
She feared they wouldn't let her chew the betel.
Should I leave my children?
How would I make a living?
What would happen when the communists came?

When I made up my mind,
pictures of my childhood floated to the surface
as clear and strong as dreams.

Our old house in Hadong.
The bamboo in the backyard.
We ate the shoots.
The soldiers made a fence from the stalks.
My sister and I painted the fence
first white, then blue, then her favorite yellow.
The small antigonon vine we planted
with its pink blossoms in spring.

Our ponds.
The many steps down
to the small bridge

where we'd sit hour after hour
letting our hands dip into the water
trying to catch the silver-brown fish.

Airplanes bombing
running from our house
people dying, people calling from outside the walls
don't take me. I'm not dead yet.
The family hiding together in our house in Cholon
sunlight coming through the bullet holes.

Picture Bride

Cathy Song

She was a year younger
than I,
twenty-three when she left Korea.
Did she simply close
the door of her father's house
and walk away. And
was it a long way
through the tailor shops of Pusan
to the wharf where the boat
waited to take her to an island
whose name she had
only recently learned,
on whose shore
 a man waited,
turning her photograph
to the light when the lanterns
in the camp outside
Waialua Sugar Mill were lit
and the inside of his room
grew luminous
from the wings of moths
migrating out of the cane stalks?
What things did my grandmother
take with her? And when
she arrived to look
into the face of the stranger
who was her husband,
thirteen years older than she,
did she politely untie
the silk bow of her jacket,
her tent-shaped dress
filling with the dry wind
that blew from the surrounding fields
where the men were burning the cane?

Blue Lantern

Cathy Song

The blue lantern light
was like a full moon
swelling above the hush
of the mock orange shrubs
that separated our houses.

It was light
from your grandfather's room.

I remember the music
at night.
I dreamed the music
came in squares,
like birthday chocolate,
through the window
on a blue plate.

From his shakuhachi,
shavings of notes,
floated, and fell;
melted where the stillness
inserted itself back into night.
It was quiet then until dawn,
broken once by a single wailing:
the sound of an animal
whose hind leg is caught in a trap.

It was your grandfather
mourning his dead wife.
He played for her each night;
her absence,
the shape of his grief
funneled through the bamboo flute.
A ritual of remembrance,
keeping her memory alive
with his old breath.

He played unknowingly
to the child next door
who lay stricken by the music
transposed to her body,
waiting for the cry
that always surprised her;
like a glimpse of shadow
darting through the room
before she would drift off into sleep.

I knew you were in the room
just beyond the music.

This was something we shared.
Listening, my eyes closed
as though I were under water
in the blueness of my room;
I felt buoyant and protected.

I imagined you, his grandson,
listening and lying
in your small bed;
your head making a slight
dent in the pillow.

It was as though the weight
of his grief washed over
the two of us
each night like a tide,
leaving our bodies beached
but unbruised,
white and firm like shells.

The Grammar of Silk

Cathy Song

On Saturdays in the morning
my mother sent me to Mrs. Umemoto's sewing school.
It was cool and airy in her basement,
pleasant—a word I choose
to use years later to describe
the long tables where we sat
and cut, pinned, and stitched,
the Singer's companionable whirr,
the crisp, clever bite of scissors
parting like silver fish a river of calico.

The school was in walking distance
to Kaimuki Dry Goods
where my mother purchased my supplies—
small cards of buttons,
zippers and rickrack packaged like licorice,
lifesaver rolls of thread
in fifty-yard lengths,
spun from spools, tough as tackle.
Seamstresses waited at the counters
like librarians to be consulted.
Pens and scissors dangled like awkward pendants
across flat chests,
a scarf of measuring tape flung across a shoulder,
time as a pincushion bristled at the wrist.
They deciphered a dress's blueprints
with an architect's keen eye.

This evidently was a sanctuary,
a place where women confined with children
conferred, consulted the oracle,
the stone tablets of the latest pattern books.

Here mothers and daughters paused in symmetry,
offered the proper reverence—
hushed murmurings for the shantung silk
which required a certain sigh,
as if it were a piece from the Ming Dynasty.

My mother knew there would be no shortcuts
and headed for the remnants,
the leftover bundles with yardage
enough for a heart-shaped pillow,
a child's dirndl, a blouse without darts.
Along the aisles
my fingertips touched the titles—
satin, tulle, velvet,
peach, lavender, pistachio,
sherbet-colored linings—
and settled for the plain brown-and-white composition
of polka dots on kettle cloth
my mother held up in triumph.

She was determined that I should sew
as if she knew what she herself was missing,
a moment when she could have come up for air—
the children asleep,
the dishes drying on the rack—
and turned on the lamp
and pulled back the curtain of sleep.
To inhabit the night,
the night as a black cloth, white paper,
a sheet of music in which she might find herself singing.

On Saturdays at Mrs. Umemoto's sewing school,
when I took my place beside the other girls,
bent my head and went to work,
my foot keeping time on the pedal,
it was to learn the charitable oblivion
of hand and mind as one—
a refuge such music affords the maker—
the pleasure of notes in perfectly measured time.

Biographical Notes

Sucheng Chan teaches Asian American studies at the University of California (Santa Barbara). She has won awards for her teaching and for her books on Asian Americans, which include *Asian Americans: An Interpretive History* and *This Bittersweet Soil: The Chinese in California Agriculture, 1860–1910*.

Diana Chang (born 1934) has written a number of novels and poetry collections. Her jobs have included teaching creative writing at Barnard College and editing *The American Pen*, a quarterly newsletter for writers.

Isabelle Chang (born 1924) has published Chinese cookbooks and collections of Chinese folk tales. In 1965, she won the John Greene Chandler medal for excellence in juvenile writing. Among other accomplishments, she speaks Chinese fluently and reads French, Italian, Spanish, and Latin.

Lan Samantha Chang earned a degree in East Asian Studies from Yale University and is a graduate of the University of Iowa Writers' Workshop. Her stories have been published in *Beloit Fiction Journal*, *The Atlantic Monthly*, and *Best American Short Stories 1994*.

Marilyn Chin has received a number of awards for her poetry, including a fellowship from the National Endowment for the Arts and the Stegner fellowship from Stanford University. Her books include *Dwarf Bamboo* and *The Phoenix Gone, The Terrace Empty*.

Alan Chong Lau (born 1948) has written, among other books, a volume of poetry entitled *Songs From Jadina*, which won an American Book Award from the Before Columbus Foundation. Jadina is the name of his grandmother, to whom the book is dedicated.

S. I. Hayakawa (1906–1992) was born of Japanese immigrant parents in Vancouver, Canada. However, he became a United States citizen, earned a Ph.D. in American literature, and represented California in the United States Senate. He is famous for his attempts to make English America's official language.

Le Ly Hayslip (born 1949) left her native Vietnam as a young woman while the Vietnam War was still raging. She put down roots in California and eventually created an organization that provides medical and educational aid to Vietnam. The director Oliver Stone based his film *Heaven and Earth* on her autobiography, *When Heaven and Earth Changed Places*.

Marlon K. Hom teaches Asian American studies at San Francisco State University. His book *Songs of Gold Mountain* contains translations of poems by Chinese immigrants who passed through San Francisco's Angel Island Immigration Station (1910–1940).

Jeanne Wakatsuki Houston (born 1934) grew up in California and, during World War II, was sent with her family to a relocation center for Japanese Americans. Years later, prompted by a question from her nephew, she decided to write about this difficult experience. She called her book about this time *Farewell to Manzanar*.

Garrett Hongo (born 1951) was born in Volcano, Hawaii, and grew up in Hawaii and the Los Angeles area. His second book of poetry, *The River of Heaven* (1988), won the Lamont prize given by the Academy of American Poets. His essay "Kubota" was selected by Joyce Carol Oates for the anthology *Best American Essays 1991*.

Lawson Fusao Inada (born 1938) was born in Fresno, California. He was the first Asian American poet to have a book published by a major American publishing company, and he edited *Aiiieeeee!: An Anthology of Asian-American Writers* (1974).

Gish Jen (born 1956), the daughter of Chinese immigrants, grew up outside of New York City. Named Lillian, she was nicknamed Gish after the actress Lillian Gish. She says that a major goal of her fiction is to have readers "see Asian Americans as 'us' rather than 'other.'"

Wendy Wilder Larsen (born 1940) lived and worked in Saigon, Vietnam, in the early 1970's. There she met Tran Thi Nga, and the two eventually collaborated on a book in verse about their experiences: *Shallow Graves: Two Women and Vietnam*.

Li-Young Lee (born 1957) was born in Indonesia of Chinese parents. His award-winning books of poetry are *Rose* and *The City in Which I Love You*. He has also written a remembrance of his father entitled *the winged seed*.

Shirley Geok-lin Lim grew up in Malaysia. Among her many books are *Crossing the Peninsula*, which won the 1980 Commonwealth Poetry Prize. She also edited *The Forbidden Stitch: An Asian American Women's Anthology*, which won an American Book Award.

Ved Mehta came to America from India. His autobiography, *Sound-Shadows of the New World*, influenced many American writers who share Mehta's South Asian roots.

Toshio Mori (1910–1980) was born in Oakland, California. During World War II, he and his family were sent to a relocation center for Japanese Americans. In 1943, he became the first Japanese American to have a story published in the Best American Short Story series. He went on to publish two collections of short stories and a novel.

Lensey Namioka (born 1929) was born in Beijing, China, but eventually settled in Seattle, Washington. She is a well-known writer of novels for young adults. *Phantom of Tiger Mountain*, for example, is a mystery set in ancient China.

Monica Sone (born 1919) is the author of the autobiography *Nisei Daughter*, from which this excerpt comes. (*Nisei* means second-generation Japanese; Sone's father emigrated to the United States in 1904.) Critics have praised this book for its vivid description of how World War II affected Japanese Americans.

Cathy Song (born 1955) was born in Honolulu, Hawaii, of a Chinese American mother and a Korean American father. She received an M.A. in creative writing from Boston University, and her first book, *Picture Bride*, was selected as the 1982 winner of the Yale Series of Younger Poets competition.

Amy Tan (born 1952), raised in Oakland, California, by her Chinese immigrant parents, began her working life as a business writer. Her novel *The Joy Luck Club* (1989) was her first published fiction book, and it was a bestseller. In addition to being translated into many languages, it inspired a movie of the same title. Tan has also written another best-selling novel entitled *The Kitchen God's Wife*.

Tran Thi Nga (born 1927) lived in Vietnam from an early age. She experienced many ordeals and had many adventures before escaping to the United States as the Vietnam War ended. *Shallow Graves: Two Women and Vietnam*, the book of verse on which she collaborated with Wendy Wilder Larsen, tells the dramatic story of her life.

Yoshiko Uchida (1921–1992) became known for her prize-winning collections of Japanese folk tales and her descriptions of the Japanese experience in the United States. Her goal, she once said, was "to give young Asians a sense of their own history" and to write about Japanese Americans so that non-Asians would see them "as real people."

Jade Snow Wong (born 1922) grew up in San Francisco's Chinatown. As a girl, she tried to learn American customs while her parents followed traditional Chinese ways. Wong tells about this period of her life in her autobiography *Fifth Chinese Daughter*, from which "Lucky to Be Born a Chinese" comes.

Belle Yang is a visual artist and a writer. In *Baba*, she uses folk tales and rumors to convey a fictional version of her father's Chinese world. As Amy Tan asserts, Yang is "an American writer who writes in English and thinks in Chinese."

Paul Yee (born 1956) grew up in Vancouver's Chinatown, where he felt "caught between two worlds and [yearned] to move away from the neighborhood." Since then, however, he has paid tribute to his Chinese roots in such books as *The Curses of Third Uncle* and *Saltwater City: An Illustrated History of the Chinese in Vancouver*.

Acknowledgments *(continued from p. ii)*

Simon & Schuster Books for Young Readers, an imprint of Simon & Schuster Children's Publishing Division, and Groundwood Books Ltd., a division of Douglas McIntyre
"Forbidden Fruit" from *Tales From Gold Mountain: Stories of the Chinese in the New World* by Paul Yee. Text copyright © 1989 by Paul Yee. Reprinted by permission.

University of California Press
From *Songs of Gold Mountain: Cantonese Rhymes from San Francisco Chinatown*, selected and translated by Marlon K. Hom. Copyright © 1987 The Regents of the University of California. Reprinted by permission of the publisher, University of California Press.

University of Pittsburgh Press
"The Grammar of Silk" from *School Figures* by Cathy Song. Copyright © 1994 by Cathy Song. Reprinted by permission of the University of Pittsburgh Press.

University of Washington Press
"Lucky to Be Born a Chinese" from *Fifth Chinese Daughter* by Jade Snow Wong. Copyright 1950, renewed 1989. Reprinted by permission of the University of Washington Press.

University Press of New England
"What For" from *Yellow Light* by Garrett Kaoru Hongo. Copyright © 1982 by Garrett Kaoru Hongo, Wesleyan University Press by permission of University Press of New England.

Washington Institute Press
Excerpt from "The Case for Official English," from *One Nation Indivisible? The English Language Amendment* by S. I. Hayakawa. Copyright © 1985 by Washington Institute for Values in Public Policy. Reprinted with permission of the publisher.

The Wylie Agency, Inc.
"Housepainting" by Lan Samantha Chang. Copyright © 1994 by Samantha Chang, first printed in *American Eyes*. From *Sound-Shadows of the New World* by Ved Mehta. Copyright © 1985 by Ved Mehta. First published in *Sound-Shadows of the New World*. Reprinted with permission of The Wylie Agency, Inc.

Yale University Press
"Picture Bride" and "Blue Lantern" from *Picture Bride* by Cathy Song. Copyright © 1983 by Cathy Song. Reprinted by permission of the publisher, Yale University Press.

Note: Every effort has been made to locate the copyright owner of material reprinted in this book. Omissions brought to our attention will be corrected in subsequent editions.